Social Science Experiments

This book is designed for an undergraduate, one-semester course in experimental research, primarily targeting programs in sociology, political science, environmental studies, psychology, and communications. Aimed at those with limited technical background, this introduction to social science experiments takes a practical, hands-on approach. After explaining key features of experimental designs, Green takes students through exercises designed to build appreciation for the nuances of design, implementation, analysis, and interpretation. Using applications and statistical examples from many social science fields, the textbook illustrates the breadth of what may be learned through experimental inquiry. A chapter devoted to research ethics introduces broader ethical considerations, including research transparency. The culminating chapter prepares readers for their own social science experiments, offering examples of studies that can be conducted ethically, inexpensively, and quickly. Replication datasets and R code for all examples and exercises are available online at cambridge.org/socialscienceexperiments.

Donald P. Green is Burgess Professor of Political Science at Columbia University. His path-breaking research uses experiments to study topics such as voting, prejudice, mass media, and gender-based violence.

T0349602

Social Science Experiments

A Hands-on Introduction

DONALD P. GREEN

Columbia University

CAMBRIDGE
UNIVERSITY PRESS

University Printing House, Cambridge CB2 8BS, United Kingdom

One Liberty Plaza, 20th Floor, New York, NY 10006, USA

477 Williamstown Road, Port Melbourne, VIC 3207, Australia

314–321, 3rd Floor, Plot 3, Splendor Forum, Jasola District Centre, New Delhi – 110025, India

103 Penang Road, #05-06/07, Visioncrest Commercial, Singapore 238467

Cambridge University Press is part of the University of Cambridge.

It furthers the University's mission by disseminating knowledge in the pursuit of education, learning, and research at the highest international levels of excellence.

www.cambridge.org
Information on this title: www.cambridge.org/9781009186971
DOI: 10.1017/9781009186957

First published 2022

Printed in the United Kingdom by TJ Books Ltd

A catalogue record for this publication is available from the British Library.

Library of Congress Cataloging-in-Publication Data
NAMES: Green, Donald P., 1961- author.
TITLE: Social science experiments : a hands-on introduction / Donald P. Green.
DESCRIPTION: Cambridge ; New York, NY : Cambridge University Press, 2022. | Includes bibliographical references. | SUMMARY: "Social Science Experiments: A Hands-on Introduction is an accessible textbook for undergraduates. Its four objectives are to help readers to (1) become perceptive critics of social science claims and the evidence used to support them, (2) learn basic terminology used to describe experimental designs and the statistical analysis of experimental data, (3) design and conduct a small-scale randomized experiment in a manner that sheds light on a causal question while at the same time respecting ethical boundaries, and (4) appreciate the importance of research transparency in all phases of experimental design and analysis. Chapters draw on a wide array of social science experiments from fields such as political science, psychology, criminology, and health. The textbook assumes no prior background in statistics or programming, making it a perfect complement for a course in introductory statistics. Worked examples are written in the open-source software R. The exercises invite readers to work with publicly-available datasets from published studies. Solutions to the exercises appear at the back of the book. Further instruction in R is provided by an R Companion to this volume"– Provided by publisher.
IDENTIFIERS: LCCN 2022003225 (print) | LCCN 2022003226 (ebook) | ISBN 9781009186971 (hardback) | ISBN 9781009186964 (paperback) | ISBN 9781009186957 (epub)
SUBJECTS: LCSH: Social sciences–Experiments–Textbooks. | Social sciences–Research–Textbooks. | Experimental design–Textbooks.
CLASSIFICATION: LCC H62 .G75122 2022 (print) | LCC H62 (ebook) | DDC 300.72–DC23/eng/20220311
LC record available at https://lccn.loc.gov/2022003225
LC ebook record available at https://lccn.loc.gov/2022003226

ISBN 978-1-009-18697-1 Hardback
ISBN 978-1-009-18696-4 Paperback

Contents

Preface

For more than twenty years, I have taught undergraduate courses on experimental design. This textbook is my attempt to write an accessible and engaging introduction for students who have little experience conducting primary research and perhaps no exposure to social science experiments. As far as I can tell, that description seems to fit the vast majority of undergraduates majoring in political science, sociology, communications, environmental studies, or history. In economics or psychology, which tend to have their own dedicated statistics courses, few students design, conduct, or analyze experiments.

Although I enjoy teaching statistics, I was determined not to let this primer on experiments turn into a statistics textbook. *Social Science Experiments: A Hands-on Introduction* attempts to convey an intuitive appreciation for experimental design. Unlike the graduate textbook that I co-authored (Gerber and Green 2012), this textbook keeps notation to a minimum and discusses only essential statistical concepts. The first six chapters attempt to build an intuitive understanding of the key design principles that make experiments instructive. The examples that suffuse this book are designed to spark students' interest. I want students to see the relevance of experimental reasoning for their everyday lives as well as their academic pursuits. Chapter 7 invites readers to do more with their data, introducing regression, graphics, and hypothesis testing.

Unlike most textbooks, this *Hands-on Introduction* urges readers to roll up their sleeves and conduct their own experiments. Chapters 3 and 6 invite students to design their own original studies. The design process is meant to prompt reflection on basic questions. What is the treatment ... and control? Who are the participants? What is the hypothesis? The process also entails creating a dataset, inspecting the results, and drawing inferences. Learning is easier when the motivation to acquire specific skills emerges organically through hands-on experience.

My four teaching objectives are to help readers to (1) become perceptive critics of social science claims and the evidence used to support them, (2) learn the basic terminology used to describe experimental designs and the statistical analysis of experimental data, (3) acquire the ability to design and conduct a small-scale randomized experiment in a manner that sheds light on a causal question while at the same time respecting ethical boundaries, and (4) appreciate the importance of research transparency in all phases of experimental design and analysis.

In keeping with the fourth objective, readers are encouraged to use open-source software and archive their materials in public repositories. This book is therefore written using elementary code for the R software language. All code and data are available from the book's open-source repository (https://osf.io/b78je/). More advanced R code may also be found there and in the online *R Companion*, available at cambridge .org/socialscienceexperiments, which provides instructional tools for those who want to learn more about data analysis.

This book may be used as the main text for a dedicated course on experiments, or it may accompany a brief experiments module within a course on research methods or introductory statistics. The many articles and datasets that I have compiled for the exercises help reinforce material from other parts of a research methods survey course.

I wish to acknowledge the many people who provided assistance during the preparation of this book. I had the good fortune of working with four outstanding undergraduate research assistants, Yesenia Ruano, Oscar Scott, Kerem Tuncer, and Alan Zhou, who contributed to every aspect of this book. This team worked tirelessly throughout the entire book-writing process, despite the fact that the COVID-19 epidemic prevented us from ever meeting in person. I am grateful to Michelle Zee, who helped prepare solution sets and R code, and Gosha Syunyaev, who served as a teaching assistant for this course while the book was in development. Special thanks go to Alex Coppock, Pia Deshpande, Jamie Druckman, Josh Kalla, Bruce Kogut, Costas Panagopoulos, Ethan Porter, Betsy Sinclair, and Gaurav Sood, who so generously commented on working drafts of this manuscript. I am indebted to the many researchers who graciously shared their data for the book's worked examples and exercises. I also owe a long-term debt to Alan Gerber, who shaped my thinking on so many topics as we co-taught courses on experimental design. Final thanks go to Columbia University, whose sabbatical leave and research support made this writing project possible.

I

Experiments as Fair Tests

Causal claims abound in everyday life. Open your medicine cabinet: Do these over-the-counter products to ameliorate headaches or bug bites actually work as advertised? Open your closet: Does your choice of wardrobe change the way that others treat you? Open your refrigerator: Did you buy nonfat milk because you hoped to lose some weight? Open today's news: Do government programs have a material effect on economic or social outcomes? Stepping back to reflect for a moment, you probably have hunches about whether these pills or products or policies change the way that things turn out.

How did you come to acquire these beliefs about cause and effect? In some cases, you may have drawn on your own experience and intuitions. Did your allergy symptoms subside when you took that hay fever medication? Without putting too much thought or effort into settling the question, a reasonable person might conclude that the medication worked because it produced an abrupt change in symptoms. Where you lacked direct personal experience, you may have drawn inferences based on other things that you know. For example, you might infer that low-fat milk will help you lose weight because it contains fewer calories than whole milk. In addition to drawing your own conclusions based on experience and logic, you may have accepted other people's causal assessments, such as recommendations by health professionals or policy evaluations by knowledgeable researchers. Your causal beliefs may reflect a combination of all three sources.

Informal empiricism sometimes works quite well. Experience is probably an adequate guide if your aim is to figure out whether staying up all night makes you drowsy the next day or whether turning on the air conditioner reduces the temperature in your room. Reasoning based on background knowledge may be a reliable guide on questions such as whether it is safe to operate a corded electrical appliance outdoors in the rain. And experts may provide reliable guidance on questions such as the share of the population that must be vaccinated in order for "herd immunity" to prevent the spread of infectious disease.

On the other hand, informal empiricism may give us false confidence in causal claims. Many people swear that eating local honey relieves seasonal allergies. In addition to offering testimonials from those whose allergy symptoms subsided after eating local honey, proponents of this hypothesis argue that this effect can be deduced from the fact that eating local pollen, which is mixed into the honey, helps allergy-sufferers build up immunities. However, skeptics question whether honey-borne pollen can be expected to help alleviate allergy symptoms. Local honey may contain the wrong kind of pollen – as one summary points out, "Bees typically pollinate colorful flowers, yet most people are allergic to pollen released by grasses, trees and weeds."[1] Informal empiricism may lead people to draw opposing conclusions about cause and effect.

We often look to experts to resolve such controversies, but experts, too, are fallible. They are often overconfident (Dawes 2009), and their pronouncements may be tinged by conflicts of interest (Tetlock 2017). For example, political campaigns in the United States spend vast sums of money on digital advertising, and consultants who sell these ads are quick to vouch for their effectiveness, pointing to campaigns that skillfully used digital ads on their way to victory. But carefully controlled experiments cast doubt on whether these ads persuade their target audience to change their vote (Broockman and Green 2014). In clinical medicine, physicians have been found to continue to perform surgical procedures even after they have been shown to be ineffective. Arthroscopy is commonly used to treat knee arthritis, despite the fact that a carefully-controlled experiment showed the procedure to be no more effective than a placebo operation (Gerber and Patashnik 2006; Siemieniuk et al. 2017). Experts also proved unable to predict which of 54 messages to encourage exercise would get gym members to visit their gym more often. A randomized trial involving more than 60,000 gym members showed that only a small number of encouragement messages produced positive results and that experts grossly overestimated the effectiveness of every message (Milkman et al. 2021).

The preceding examples underscore the importance of research design when adjudicating questions of cause and effect. Take the example of SAT preparatory courses. Full-blown courses can be quite expensive, and each year the test-prep industry takes in billions of dollars. What evidence suggests that in-person classes or online instruction raises SAT scores substantially? First, test-prep companies point out that those who take the courses typically receive much higher scores than those who do not. The superior performance of course-takers bolsters the intuition that hard work preparing for the test pays off. But skeptics question this interpretation, pointing out that high-achieving high school students are more likely to enroll in a prep course than those with less distinguished academic records. Even if the courses truly had no effect on SAT scores, we would still expect higher scores among those who enroll in these courses than those who do not. A second body of evidence shows that those who spend more hours studying for the SAT receive higher scores than their counterparts who spend fewer hours. Again, skeptics object that high-achieving students tend to invest long hours in test preparation, so, even if studying had no effect on scores, we would expect higher scores among those who studied extensively. A third body of evidence suggests that SAT scores are higher among people who take prep courses than among those who do not, even when the comparison focuses solely on high school students with similar grades and from similar schools. This type of detailed comparison is more persuasive than a coarse comparison

---

[1] Quoted in www.aentassociates.com/raw-local-honey-cure-allergies/ (last accessed June 8, 2021). The scientific evidence is at best mixed. One study conducted in Connecticut (Rajan et al. 2002) found local honey to have no effects on allergy symptoms; another in Malaysia (Asha'ari et al. 2013) found equivocal evidence. I thank Dr. David Gudis and Dr. Stephen Canfil for their insights into the theory and evidence concerning this hypothesis.

of those who do or do not take prep classes, but it still leaves room for skepticism. Why did certain high school students take the prep class? Two students from the same school can have the same grades but different levels of ability or motivation. If the more able or motivated are more likely to take the prep course than their counterparts, the course may appear to work even if it truly has no effect. A fourth body of evidence focuses on the fact that students who enroll in a prep course after receiving a disappointing initial SAT score tend to do better on their second try at the test. Test prep companies point to this pattern as proof that their courses boost test scores. Skeptics, however, point out that this pattern merely reflects the fact that people who receive disappointing scores will, on average, score higher next time (just as people who are surprised to receive strong scores will tend to do worse if they retake the exam). Finally, what about evidence showing that, among people who received the same initial SAT score, those who took a prep course before taking the test again tended to score higher on their second try than those who did not take a course? Same problem, says the skeptic. Imagine two people with the same initial score. Disappointed and expecting to improve, one student takes a prep course; satisfied and perhaps a bit complacent, the other student does not. Even if the course truly has no effect on the second test, one might still expect the first student to receive a higher score than the second student.

Notice that the back-and-forth between prep course proponents and skeptics has a recurrent theme. Any evidence that proponents offer will be rejected by skeptics on the grounds that those who take preparatory courses have higher scholastic aptitude to begin with than those who do not take the courses.

What kind of evidence would satisfy a determined skeptic? Presumably, the skeptic wants to see what happens when students' scholastic aptitude is unrelated to whether they take a prep course or not. In that case, the skeptic cannot complain that those who took the course were more able or motivated to begin with. But where would we find such a comparison?

One approach is to compare students who decided to take the class or not, focusing just on the students who seem to share identical background attributes. They appear to have the same grades; they come from the same schools; their parents have the same educational credentials; and so on. On the surface, those who took the prep classes look just like those who did not. But the skeptic still wonders whether these two groups are truly similar. Yes, they may have the same observed attributes, but what about the attributes that were not measured, such as their level of motivation? Very well, suppose researchers were to measure students' motivation, perhaps by administering a survey, and focus the comparison even more narrowly on those who seem to have the same level of motivation. Nevertheless, other attributes remain unmeasured, such as the encouragement they receive from their peers. Even when presented with "big data" – a study involving vast numbers of students and copious information about each student's background – the skeptic will continue to wonder whether there remains some unmeasured attribute that leads certain students to enroll in prep courses and perform especially well on the SAT.

An alternative approach, and the focus of this book, is to randomly assign students to either take an SAT prep class or not. For example, many high school students want to take a prep course but come from families that cannot afford to pay for it. Imagine that these eager students enroll in a lottery and winners receive tuition-free admission to prep classes immediately. Both groups receive free admission to an SAT test to be administered three months from now. Suppose that all the lottery applicants (both winners and losers) take this test. And suppose that the lottery winners indeed attend their prep course, while the lottery losers prepare as they ordinarily would, without the benefit of a course. Would this research design satisfy a determined skeptic? The skeptic's earlier objection stemmed from the concern that students ordinarily self-select into taking a prep course, but in this research design, known as a *randomized experiment*, luck of the draw differentiates lottery winners from the lottery losers. Assuming the lottery is conducted honestly, there is no reason to expect that more gifted or determined students will win admission to the test-prep course. By chance, one group might be more determined or gifted than the other before the class begins, but there is no reason to expect the lottery winners to have more scholastic aptitude than the lottery losers.

Experiments are characterized as fair tests because, when the experimental groups are formed by chance, neither group has a head start over the other. In this example, if the group that attended the prep course received higher average scores than the group that did not attend the prep course, the skeptic must come to grips with this stubborn fact. Of course, the skeptic may still harbor doubts. No experiment is perfect. Were the lottery losers demoralized because they were unable to enroll in a prep course? Perhaps higher scores among the lottery winners reflect not the benefits of the course per se but demoralization among the lottery losers? Or perhaps by chance more able students were selected as lottery winners? Conducting a fair test does not necessarily end debate, but now the scope of debate narrows considerably. Anticipating the criticism that lottery losers become demoralized, a researcher could conduct a survey of all lottery participants shortly before the exam. If morale appears to be the same among lottery winners and losers, this criticism seems unfounded. If the concern is that random chance assigned especially able students to the test-prep group, this conjecture can be evaluated statistically using the methods described in the chapters that follow. Or researchers can repeat the experiment until the it-happened-by-chance conjecture becomes untenable. Eventually, fair tests will home in on the answer to the question of whether SAT prep classes work. As experimental evidence mounts, it will also shed light on the question of how well they work, for whom, and under what conditions.

Experiments are especially important when the "treatment" – a pill, a prep course, an experience – is something that people ordinarily select for themselves. Consider the experiment conducted by Balcells et al. (2022) on the effects of bringing Chilean university students to the Museum of Memory and Human Rights, which memorializes victims of General Augusto Pinochet's dictatorship in Chile. Students who had not previously visited the museum were invited to meet on campus and were randomly assigned to visit the museum or simply complete an exit survey. Before attending the museum, the 126 students who later attended the museum expressed the same average level of support for military rule as the 106 students in the control group. When all participants were reinterviewed a week later, 17 percent of students who attended the museum supported military rule, as compared to 28 percent of their control group counterparts, a difference of 11 percentage points.

What if this study had not randomly assigned students to visit the museum, but instead simply surveyed those who attended the museum? First, absent a control group, it would not be clear what their level of support for military dictatorship should be compared to. Second, absent random assignment to treatment and control, it would be unclear whether the museum experience was a cause of attitude change. For example, a survey that merely compared the opinions of people who attended the Museum of Memory and Human Rights to the opinions of people who attended a nearby art museum would leave us wondering whether people with different views about military rule chose to go to different museums.

1.1 AN OVERVIEW OF THIS BOOK

The chapters that lie ahead are written with several goals in mind. The first is to urge you to think critically about the causal claims that you encounter in everyday life. What evidence supports or refutes a causal claim? The second goal is to convey a sense of why experiments often provide convincing evidence about cause-and-effect. Why are experiments so often characterized as the "gold standard" for evaluating whether an intervention is effective? The third goal is to prepare you to read experiments that illuminate important cause-and-effect relationships in psychology, education, politics, economics, health, crime, media studies, and many other fields. The fourth goal is to appreciate the limitations of an experimental design or the way an experiment was implemented. What changes would have made the study more convincing or useful? The final goal is to inspire you to look at the world from an experimental vantage point. When the time comes to make an informed decision, you may need to read or conduct an experiment, and this book helps you think about the ingredients that make for an informative experimental design.

To make the material come to life, this book takes a hands-on approach. To consolidate your understanding of the material, you will be conducting your own experiments. Chapter 2 lays out the key ideas that inform an experimental design, and Chapter 3 gives you an opportunity to design, implement, and analyze a small product-testing experiment. Chapter 4 provides a panorama of social science experiments conducted in a variety of countries on topics ranging from reducing prejudice to preventing deforestation. Chapter 5 lays out ethical issues to consider before conducting an experiment involving human participants. Chapter 6 walks you through the process of planning a social science experiment, implementing the experimental design, and addressing contingencies that may arise during data collection. This chapter also guides you through the process of writing up your statistical analysis and archiving your experimental materials when your study is complete. Chapter 7 invites you to learn some graphical and statistical methods that will enable you to do more with your data. If you are reading this book as part of a statistics course, experiments will help deepen your understanding of statistics, and vice versa.

2

Key Terms

This chapter introduces key terms used to describe experiments and, more generally, the investigation of cause and effect. Because so many different disciplines use experiments, layers of overlapping terminology have accumulated, and this chapter tries to cut through the clutter by grouping synonyms, thereby keeping jargon to a minimum. In addition to providing definitions, this chapter explains why these key concepts are important in practice.

This chapter aspires to be more than a glossary of terms. It presents definitions in a logical sequence that starts with the basic ingredients of an experiment (treatments, outcomes), takes up the question of what we mean by a causal effect, and then builds to the core assumptions on which experiments depend.

2.1 TREATMENT OR INTERVENTION

In biomedical research, the term *treatment* refers to a medical procedure or pharmaceutical product whose effects are to be evaluated. For example, one might want to know whether a specific type of stomach reduction surgery known as gastric bypass leads to long-term weight loss. Briefly put, this surgery reduces the size of the stomach so that patients will feel full sooner when eating. Medical professionals have described this treatment in great length, even going so far as to film the procedure.[1]

When describing any treatment, it is important to clarify what counts as the absence of treatment. For example, will gastric bypass surgery be contrasted with another surgical procedure designed to promote weight loss? Or contrasted with a sham surgery that does not affect the digestive tract? Or contrasted with no surgery at all? This clarification about the *control* condition can have important implications for the design of the study and the interpretation of the results. If we contrast gastric bypass surgery with sham surgery (assuming the patient is unaware of which kind of surgery actually took place), we are testing the physiological effects of this specific procedure while holding constant the psychological effects of believing that one has undergone a

---

[1] See https://asmbs.org/patients/bariatric-surgery-procedures (last accessed June 10, 2021).

stomach reduction operation. Studies of this kind are called *placebo–control trials* because the inactive placebo leads subjects to believe that they are receiving the treatment. The administration of a placebo also allows the researcher to compare only people who demonstrate a willingness to undergo surgery; some of these subjects receive gastric bypass surgery, and others receive sham surgery.

On the other hand, if we contrast gastric bypass surgery to no surgery whatsoever, we reveal the combined physiological and psychological effects of the procedure, assuming everyone who is slated to receive a gastric bypass actually goes through with the surgical procedure. Usually, biomedical researchers are primarily interested in the physiological effects of a surgical procedure, not the psychological effects of undergoing any surgery, such as a sham surgery in which the patient is sedated, an incision is made, and the wound is stitched back together.[2]

The term "treatment" is used outside the domain of biomedical research to refer to a wide array of interventions whose effects are the object of study. Here are some illustrative examples of interventions that have been studied by social scientists:

- Economists study the effects of social programs that provide cash assistance to the poor (Baird et al. 2014). The intervention is the new program of cash assistance, and the control group receives only the usual support from social welfare programs.
- Criminologists study the effects of increased police surveillance in high-crime neighborhoods (Collazos et al. 2021). The intervention is a large increase in the amount of time that police patrols spend in designated locations; the control locations receive the usual level of police presence.
- Psychologists study the effects of an online diversity training program for corporate employees (Chang et al. 2019). The intervention group is exposed to an hourlong online training; the control group does not receive this training (but may be exposed to the training sometime in the future).
- Political scientists study the effects of mailings designed to encourage people to vote in an election (Panagopoulos 2011). The intervention in this case is a letter that urges registered voters who have voted in the past to cast a ballot in the upcoming election and thanks them for voting in a recent election. The control group receives no letter.[3]

Notice that in some cases the interventions are very specific – a particular diversity training program or a particular get-out-the-vote mailer. In other cases, the intervention is characterized in general terms. Increased police surveillance in the Collazos et al. (2021) study meant that, on average, police spent 50 percent more time in treated locations than they did in untreated locations, but the actual increment of police attention varied from one treated location to the next. In other words, interventions may be defined narrowly and implemented in a homogeneous manner, or they may be

---

[2] Their preference for placebo-control designs may also reflect a practical consideration. If patients slated to receive surgery frequently decide not to go through with it, the no-surgery-control design introduces an additional layer of complexity because it is unclear which subjects in the control group would have gone through with the surgery had they been slated to receive it. This kind of "failure-to-treat" problem falls outside the scope of this book but is discussed at length in chapter 5 of Gerber and Green (2012).

[3] This study also had another control group that received a letter reminding voters of the upcoming election but made no reference to past participation. See Exercise 2.3.

defined more loosely so that the treatment refers to a set of interventions that share the same basic characteristics (for example, they all involve cash transfers).

2.2 SUBJECTS OR PARTICIPANTS

Every social experiment involves some set of observations, whether they be people, firms, schools, media markets, or countries. When the observations are people, they are traditionally called *subjects*, although many researchers nowadays refer to them as *participants*.[4] In the get-out-the-vote study, the subjects are registered voters. Researchers send some subjects a "thank you for voting" mailing and assess whether this intervention makes them more likely to vote than the control group that receives no mail.

In other experiments, determining who the subjects are may be a bit tricky. In the policing study, one might say that the subjects are block-long stretches of road called street segments. Some segments receive extra police attention, while others receive the usual amount, and the question is whether additional police surveillance causes the treatment segments to experience less crime than the control segments. However, when we change the focus to how residents of treated and untreated segments feel about crime, one might think of the residents as subjects; some residents have been treated with extra police presence and others not. This example calls attention to a subtlety: In order to discern who or what the subjects are, we must first specify what the experimental outcomes are. A study with a variety of outcomes might have more than one set of subjects.

2.3 OUTCOMES

When researchers conduct experiments, they often do so with a concrete outcome in mind. For example, to what extent do get-out-the-vote mailings increase the rate at which recipients vote? In this case, the mailings constitute the treatment, and voting constitutes the outcome. Every participant in this study is associated with an outcome, either "voted" or "did not vote."

Sometimes the task of measuring outcomes requires an extra step: moving from an idealized outcome to an outcome that can be measured in practice. For example, researchers might wonder how cash transfers to poor families affect health outcomes. Are children whose families receive cash subsidies healthier than those whose families receive no special assistance? The outcome is health, but what does it mean to be healthy? One can imagine a variety of definitions, such as physical vigor or the absence of disease, and scholars actively debate the merits of competing definitions.

But even if researchers could agree on a single definition, there remains the challenge of measuring health. For example, if health were defined as the absence of disease, how extensively would researchers have to search for disease before declaring it to be absent? The constraints of time and money often dictate what researchers can measure in practice. Some studies of cash transfers simply measure the height and weight of each child as a *proxy* for health. Here, the term proxy refers to a stand-in for the underlying outcome variable that

---

[4] The term "subjects" may also refer to nonhuman participants, such as plants or products. Subjects are also referred to as *units* or *observations*.

Box 2.1 Methods to Assess Whether a Proxy Adequately Measures an Underlying Concept

When social scientists assess the validity of an outcome measure, they are evaluating whether a proposed measure gauges a particular underlying concept and nothing more. For example, the validity of the body mass index (BMI) as a measure of health boils down to whether an increase in health implies an increase in BMI and whether a decrease in health implies a decrease in BMI.

Social scientists typically use three methods for validating outcome measures:

The first is to assess the *face validity* of the measure. Does the measure bear an intuitive relationship to the underlying concept? In the case of BMI, it makes intuitive sense that a person who contracts a debilitating illness that prevents them from eating will experience declining body mass. On the other hand, one can also think of intuitive scenarios in which a person becomes morbidly obese, in which case they are less healthy but higher in BMI. The face validity of BMI as a health measure is therefore ambiguous.

Second, *criterion validity* considers whether the proposed measure confirms the judgements of experts or other carefully calibrated measures. For example, suppose one were to gather a set of people whom physicians declare to be very ill and another set whom physicians declare to be in excellent health. Would the first group have low BMI scores and the second group have high BMI scores? One reason why BMI is thought to be a valid measure of health among children in low-income countries is that, in these locations, BMI scores tend to coincide with physicians' assessments based on extensive medical examinations.

Third, *discriminant validity* asks whether the proposed measure is distinct from concepts that are not the intended target of measurement. For example, in a location where different ethnic groups tend to differ in height, BMI might reflect ethnicity rather than health. This evidence might call into question the validity of the BMI measure, or it might imply that BMI is valid when comparing members from a given ethnic group but is not valid when comparing people from different ethnic groups.

Finally, even when measures are valid, they may nonetheless contain some degree of measurement error. For example, a tape measure is a valid indicator of length (why?), but in practice those who use tape measures make errors when reading or transcribing numbers.

---

the researcher seeks to measure. When reading experimental research, it is important to attend to the distinction between the concepts that researchers strive to measure and the proxies that they use as actual measures. Whether a proxy convincingly measures the underlying concept of interest is a matter of interpretation. See Box 2.1 for a summary of methods to assess whether a proxy adequately measures an underlying concept.

When assembling the data from an actual study, a researcher records the outcome for each subject. For example, a study on cash subsidies and health may record the body mass index (BMI) for each child.[5] For concreteness, consider the outcomes for five children from different households. Two children are from families that received cash and three from families that did not, as shown in Table 2.1. As you inspect this table,

---

[5] In the metric system, BMI is defined as weight in kilograms divided by height in meters squared. To calculate BMI using imperial measures, the formula is `bmi <- (weight_pounds/height_inches^2)*703`.

TABLE 2.1. *Hypothetical schedule of potential outcomes for five subjects*

Subject no.	(1) Observed treatment	(2) Observed outcome	(3) Treated potential outcome*: $Y(1)$	(4) Untreated potential outcome*: $Y(0)$	(5) Treatment effect**	(6) Covariate: BMI measured 1 year earlier
1	1	16	16	11	5	13
2	1	20	20	12	8	12
3	0	25	25	25	0	24
4	0	29	27	29	−2	28
5	0	18	22	18	4	23
			Average $Y(1)$	Average $Y(0)$	ATE	Average covariate
			22	19	3	20
			Boxed entries observed*	Boxed entries observed*	No entries observed**	

Average outcome among those treated: 18
Average outcome among those not treated: 24
Difference-in-means estimate: −6

notice that the BMI outcomes tend to be lower for children in families that received cash subsidies. Did the cash subsidy somehow make children smaller? Or did cash tend to go to families whose children were smaller to begin with? In order to distinguish the effect of cash subsidies on BMI from the apparent relationship between cash subsidies and BMI, we must first clarify what we mean by a treatment effect. To do so, we introduce the concept of potential outcomes.

2.4 POTENTIAL OUTCOMES

When we observe an outcome for a participant who received the treatment, we might wonder what would we have observed if this participant had not received the treatment? Conversely, when we observe an outcome for an untreated participant, we might wonder what would their outcome have been had they been treated? Unfortunately, we cannot observe participants in both their treated and untreated states; we can only observe one or the other. Still, we can imagine that every participant has two potential outcomes, one that would be expressed if they were treated and another that would be expressed if they were not treated. The *causal effect of a treatment for a given subject is the difference between these two potential outcomes.*

In order to get a clearer sense of the mapping between potential outcomes and observed outcomes, return to Table 2.1. Column (3) indicates the potential BMI outcomes that subjects would express if they were treated, and column (4) indicates the potential BMI outcomes that subjects would express if they were untreated. *In practice, researchers never get to see both of these columns; the numbers in Table 2.1 are offered as a hypothetical example to clarify some important concepts.* The five entries in boxes indicate the outcomes that are actually observed, reflecting whether a given participant actually received the treatment. Column (5) lists the causal effect for each participant. Notice that, for each row, column (5) is just the difference between the treated potential outcome in column (3) and the untreated potential outcome in column (4).

2.5 AVERAGE TREATMENT EFFECT

The average treatment effect (ATE) is the average of the causal effects for all subjects.

Three noteworthy features of the ATE are illustrated in Table 2.1. First, the ATE may be calculated by computing the average of the causal effects for each subject, shown in column (5). In this example, the average of column (5) is 3. Second, the ATE can be calculated in an equivalent way: Subtract the average untreated potential outcome (19) from the average treated potential outcome (22) to obtain 3. The ATE in this illustration is positive, indicating that, on average, cash subsidies would increase the body mass of these children. Third, notice that although the average effect of the treatment is positive, it need not be positive for every child. In this example, Subject #4 has a lower treated potential outcome than untreated potential outcome and thus loses body mass if treated.

The ATE in Table 2.1 can be thought of as a hidden quantity that summarizes how these participants' outcomes would change, on average, if they all went from being untreated to being treated. Most experiments in the social sciences are designed to uncover the average treatment effect.[6]

2.6 COMPARING AVERAGE OUTCOMES OF TREATED AND UNTREATED PARTICIPANTS

Except in special cases, researchers do not know the true value of the average treatment effect.[7] Instead, they must use the data they collect to make informed guesses about the quantity of interest, in this case the ATE. The process of making guesses is known as *estimation*. Quite often, researchers rely on a statistical procedure, or *estimator*, to generate guesses. The specific guess that an estimator produces is known as an *estimate*. The quantity of interest is called the *estimand*.

For example, a simple algorithm to estimate the ATE is to calculate the average outcome among treated subjects and subtract the average outcome among untreated subjects.[8] Averages are sometimes called means, so this estimator is known as *difference-in-means*.

---

[6] In this example, the focus is on the ATE among the participants in this particular study. Sometimes researchers have a more ambitious goal of estimating the average treatment effect in some other group, often called a *target population*. Depending on the researcher's aspirations, the target population might refer to people living in a particular country or something broader, such as people living in low-income countries, either now or sometime in the future. When we refer to the ATE, we will be referring to the average effect among the participants in the study. When we want to refer to the average treatment effect in some target population, we will use the term "population average treatment effect" (PATE).

[7] One special case is when the outcome occurs before the treatment. Assuming no one had advance knowledge of the treatment, the treatment effect is zero for every subject and the average treatment effect is also zero.

[8] Most research designs in the social sciences are termed *between-subjects designs*, because they compare treated and untreated observations at a given point in time. Less common are *within-subjects designs*, which compare a given observation over time as it moves from an untreated state to a treated state (or vice versa).

Whether an estimator such as difference-in-means offers useful insights about the ATE will depend on the research design. As we explain in Section 2.7, the difference-in-means estimator has attractive statistical properties when groups are formed by random assignment. When, on the other hand, groups are formed through some unknown process, the difference-in-means estimator may perform abysmally. Our running BMI example has focused on an instance in which subjects' access to treatment was not under the control of the researcher. What makes this running example interesting is that the ATE here is positive (treatment increases BMI by an average of 3), but the observed results show that outcomes were lower for the treated children than the untreated children. The average BMI among treated children is 18, while the average BMI among untreated children is 24. The difference-in-means estimate is −6.

What is going on? Why is this estimate so different from the actual ATE? Close inspection of Table 2.1 reveals that children with especially low potential outcomes received the treatment, while children with especially high potential outcomes were untreated. Because we do not know how subjects came to be treated, we can only speculate about why this happened. Could it be that subsidies were directed to especially needy families?

2.7 RANDOM ASSIGNMENT OF SUBJECTS TO TREATMENT

When researchers have no control over the allocation of treatments, subjects may self-select into treatment, or policymakers may direct treatments at certain types of people. Whenever exposure to the treatment is outside the researcher's control, there is the risk that treatment may be systematically related to potential outcomes. As the cash subsidy example illustrates, lower average scores among those who receive the treatment might mean that the treatment decreases outcomes, but it could instead mean that the treatment went to subjects who had low potential outcomes to begin with.

Random assignment refers to a reproducible procedure that allocates subjects to treatment with known probability that is greater than zero (i.e., each subject has some positive probability of being assigned to treatment) and less than one (i.e., each subject has some positive probability of being assigned to control). In practice, random assignment may be conducted by flipping a coin, drawing cards from a deck, or some other physical process; usually, researchers rely on computer software so that the process of assignment is both transparent and reproducible. That way, if a skeptic wants to confirm that the random assignment procedure was in fact random, the computer code helps allay doubts.

Under random assignment, potential outcomes are *statistically independent* of the assigned treatment. By statistically independent, we mean that knowing a subject's assignment gives no clues about the value of that subject's potential outcomes (and vice versa). A given random assignment might place more people with high (or low) potential outcomes into the treatment group, but over multiple experiments there will be no systematic pattern to the assignments. When using random assignment, we have no reason to suspect high (or low) potential outcomes to be associated with assignment to treatment. The treatment group is a random sample of the entire pool of subjects.

Although it is possible for a random assignment to come out exactly like the first two columns of Table 2.1, this is just one possible random assignment that allocates exactly two of the five subjects to the treatment group. Here is the list of all 10 possible assignments, where 1 indicates treatment and 0 indicates control:

	[,1]	[,2]	[,3]	[,4]	[,5]	[,6]	[,7]	[,8]	[,9]	[,10]
1	1	1	1	1	0	0	0	0	0	0
2	1	0	0	0	1	1	1	0	0	0
3	0	1	0	0	1	0	0	1	1	0
4	0	0	1	0	0	1	0	1	0	1
5	0	0	0	1	0	0	1	0	1	1

Over all possible random assignments, the average potential outcomes among those assigned to treatment will be identical to the average potential outcomes among those assigned to control.

To illustrate this point, let's take a close look at the set of all possible random assignments from an experiment that allocates exactly two out of five subjects to treatment. Notice that every subject appears in the treatment group in exactly 4 of 10 possible random assignments. In other words, this random assignment procedure gives every subject an identical chance of receiving the treatment.

The estimate we obtain from any given experiment depends on which subjects happened to be allocated randomly to the treatment group. Here is a list of estimated ATEs from each of the 10 possible random assignments, sorted from smallest to largest:

{-6, -3, -0.67, 0.83, 3.17, 3.17, 5.5, 6.17, 8.5, 12.33}

The average of these 10 estimates is 3, which correctly matches the average treatment effect of cash subsidies on BMI in Table 2.1. Why did random assignment, on average, reveal the correct answer? Because the treatment group is a random sample of all the subjects in the study, the average treated potential outcome revealed in the treatment group is expected to match that of the subject pool as a whole. Similarly, the control group is a random sample of all the subjects in the study, so the average untreated potential outcome revealed in the control group is expected to match that of the subject pool as a whole.

An estimator that, on average, yields the correct answer is said to be *unbiased*. In Section 2.9, we will say more about the concept of unbiasedness, but for now the important thing is that random assignment help create fair comparisons that, on average, reveal the true average treatment effect.

2.8 COVARIATES

A *covariate* is some form of background information that is measured prior to random assignment and thus cannot be affected by treatment. This background information might refer to attributes of the participants (e.g., their ages) or to attributes of the settings in which the experiment takes place (e.g., public schools or private schools).

Covariates can be helpful in three ways. First, covariates allow researchers to confirm that random assignment produced treatment and control groups that have similar background attributes. The treatment and control groups rarely have identical profiles, but one can assess whether background attributes differ more than would be expected by chance, given all the ways that the random assignment could have turned out. Sometimes this comparison reveals a flaw in the way that the randomization was carried out or in the way that the researcher is constructing the comparison between treatment and control.[9]

Second, covariates may help improve the precision with which the difference-in-means estimator assesses the ATE. Returning to Table 2.1, notice the rightmost column, which lists the BMI for each subject 1 year prior to the random assignment. When covariates are measured prior to random assignment they cannot be affected by treatment. If the treatment and control groups have different past BMI scores, it must be due to random chance. One way to make use of this extra information about subjects is to redefine our outcome measure as the change in BMI from the initial (pre-treatment) reading to the post-treatment reading. Because the pre-treatment BMI reading strongly predicts BMI at the end of the study, the analysis of *change scores* makes our estimate of the ATE much more precise. Over all 10 possible random assignments, the average estimate generated by the change score estimator is 3 because the change score estimator, like the difference-in-means estimator, is unbiased. But the change score estimator produces estimates that tend to be much closer to 3. Here are the 10 estimates from all possible random assignments, sorted from lowest to highest.

```
{-0.67, 0.33, 0.33, 2.33, 2.33, 3.33, 3.5, 5.5, 6.5, 6.5}
```

If you compare this list to the list generated by the difference-in-means estimator, you can confirm that the estimates are now distributed more tightly around 3. In sum, *covariates that strongly predict outcomes help researchers estimate the ATE more precisely*. This principle helps explain why researchers often attempt to obtain a baseline measure of the outcome prior to administering the treatment.

Third, covariates allow researchers to investigate the possibility that treatment effects vary from one subgroup to another. For example, one could estimate the average treatment effect separately for people under 30 years old and for people who are 30 or older. In effect, covariates allow researchers to partition an experiment into a collection of miniature experiments that can help describe the conditions under which the treatment is especially (in)effective. Understanding which kinds of subjects are especially responsive to treatment can help policymakers distribute treatments efficiently. In extreme cases, where some people experience benefit from the treatment while others are harmed, this kind of investigation can call attention to the importance of targeting only those who are likely to benefit from the intervention.

---

[9] The statistical topic of hypothesis testing addresses this question. The "null" hypothesis to be tested is that random assignment generated the observed covariate profiles of the treatment and control groups. The alternative hypothesis is that random assignment was not used or properly implemented. See Chapters 3 and 7.

2.9 SAMPLING DISTRIBUTIONS, UNBIASEDNESS, AND STANDARD ERRORS

When reading about an experiment, it is helpful to think of the results as just one draw from the set of possible random assignments. The collection of estimates that could have been obtained from all possible random assignments is known as the *sampling distribution*. Like any distribution, a sampling distribution has a mean (or average). An *unbiased* estimator is an estimator that produces a sampling distribution whose mean is the target estimand; any given estimate may be too high or too low, but this estimator on average produces the correct answer.

Another important property of the sampling distribution is how dispersed it is. A common way to describe dispersion is the *standard deviation*.[10] The larger the standard deviation, the farther the typical observation is from the mean. The standard deviation of a sampling distribution is called the *standard error*. For example, in Section 2.7 we displayed the sampling distribution of difference-in-means estimates across all 10 possible random assignments. Using R, we can describe the properties of this sampling distribution:

```
sampling_distribution <- c(-6,-3,-0.67,0.83,3.17,3.17,5.5,6.17,8.5,12.33)
```

We can confirm that its mean is 3:

```
mean(sampling_distribution)
[1]  3
```

The standard error is the square root of the average squared difference between each entry and the mean:

```
> sqrt(mean((sampling_distribution - mean(sampling_distribution))^2))
[1]  5.184915
```

The standard error of 5.18 may be thought of as the typical misprediction that an experiment of this kind will make when estimating the true ATE.

A small standard error implies that mispredictions will tend to be small, which in turn means that the estimated ATE will tend to be close to the true ATE. In an effort to drive down the standard error, researchers may try to recruit more experimental subjects. Another way to reduce the standard error is to make use of covariates that strongly predict outcomes, such as baseline measures of the outcome. In our running example, when we focus on change scores (current BMI minus BMI at baseline), the sampling distribution again has a mean of 3, but now the standard error is much smaller:

```
> sampling_dist_change_score <- c(-0.67, 0.33, 0.33, 2.33, 2.33, 3.33, 3.5, 5.5, 6.5, 6.5)

> sqrt(mean((sampling_dist_change_score - mean(sampling_dist_change_score))^2))
[1]  2.444041
```

The typical misprediction is now just 2.44. The analysis of change scores allows us to estimate the ATE more precisely (i.e., the estimates do not vary as much from one random assignment to the next).

---

[10] The standard deviation is the square root of the average squared deviation from the mean.

2.10 THREE CORE ASSUMPTIONS FOR UNBIASED ESTIMATION OF THE ATE

Under what conditions will the difference-in-means estimator produce unbiased estimates of the ATE? Three core assumptions must be satisfied.

1. *Random Assignment*: The assignment of observations to treatment and control is independent of their potential outcomes.

What kinds of implementation problems might upend random assignment? Those administering the random allocation may do so in ways that are not truly random. For example, those in charge of administering a medical trial might want to see the sickest patients receive the experimental treatment; if subjects are randomly allocated to treatment in a specific order, the administrators might switch the queuing of subjects so that sicker patients are more likely to receive the treatment. The history of biomedical trials includes some infamous cases of this kind of tampering (Torgerson and Torgerson 2008, chapter 5).

Another threat to random assignment is attrition, or failure to obtain outcomes for all subjects. Attrition can occur in many ways; for example, subjects could move away or refuse to participate further in the study. Attrition jeopardizes the random assignment assumption because it raises the possibility that subjects in the treatment and control groups drop out for different reasons, so that the remaining subjects in treatment and control no longer have comparable potential outcomes.

2. *Noninterference*: Each subject's potential outcomes reflect only whether that subject is treated or not. A subject's potential outcomes are not affected by the treatments that other subjects receive.

In some experiments, this assumption seems plausible. If the treatment is exposure to a coffee advertisement that appears when one visits a website, one's purchase decision is presumably unaffected by whether others receive the advertisement or not.

In other cases, noninterference may be jeopardized by communication, displacement, or competition for resources.

- Communication: If subjects in the treatment group who receive a mailer encouraging them to vote show the mailer to their friends or neighbors in the control group, the difference-in-means estimator may tend to understate the apparent effects of the treatment.
- Displacement: In the policing experiment mentioned in Section 2.1, streets assigned to treatment received greater police surveillance than the control streets. If police presence pushes crime from treated streets to untreated streets, the difference-in-means estimator will tend to exaggerate the benefits of the treatment.
- Competition for resources: If poor families in the treatment group receive cash subsidies, their increased demand for food may drive up prices for poor families in the control group. The difference-in-means estimator may exaggerate the health benefits of cash subsidies if the control group is made worse off.

3. *Symmetry*: The treatment is the only causative factor that differs systematically between the treatment and control group; apart from the intended treatment, the two groups are treated symmetrically.

Again, intuition suggests that this requirement will be met for many experiments. If one sends a letter encouraging voting, the letter is the only factor that differs between treatment and control groups.

Common threats to the symmetry assumption include compound treatments, different administrative procedures for treatment and control subjects, and different measurement procedures for gathering outcomes.

- Compound treatment: Sometimes the content of the treatment includes multiple elements, making it impossible to isolate the effect of one specific aspect of the treatment. For example, researchers sought to assess the effects of "report cards" that graded each elected official in an Indian state legislature according to whether they showed up for votes or floor debates. The report cards were featured prominently in a local newspaper that was distributed to constituents (Banerjee et al. 2011). However, constituents living in areas that received the newspapers were also targeted with other interventions, such as local gatherings designed to publicize the records of local elected officials. The difference-in-means estimator cannot isolate the specific effects of newspaper report cards, since the treatment group received both newspapers and community gatherings.
- Different administrative procedures: Symmetry may be jeopardized when researchers use different data collection methods for treatment and control subjects. For example, researchers might send classroom observers to monitor an experimental intervention that involves a "flipped classroom" (self-guided instruction by students) for some classes and not others. If observers are dispatched only to flipped classrooms but not traditional classrooms, the difference-in-means estimator will pick up not just the effect of the flipped classroom but also the presence of outside observers.
- Different outcome measurement: The same concern holds when outcomes are measured in one way for the treatment group and another way for the control group. For example, symmetry may be violated if the post-treatment surveys for treatment and control groups are worded differently or are administered in different ways. Another common measurement concern has to do with whether raters are aware of subjects' treatment status. For example, when physicians look for symptoms of a disease that is thought to be prevented by an experimental vaccine, do they know which subjects received the vaccine as opposed to the placebo? Researchers often make special efforts to *blind* raters from knowing which subjects were treated and to *blind* participants from knowing the purpose of the study, so that the outcomes they express reflect exposure to the treatment rather than their desire to confirm what they take to be the researcher's hypothesis. Studies that do both are said to use a *double-blind* design.

Assessing whether these three core assumptions are met is a matter of judgment and requires close inspection of an experimental design. For this reason, it is crucial that experimental researchers describe their designs in sufficient detail to allow readers to assess each assumption.

When all three assumptions are met, the difference-in-means estimator generates unbiased estimates of the ATE. For a proof of this theorem and a corresponding theorem that shows that the difference-in-change-score estimator is unbiased, see

Appendix 2.1. This theorem has an important take-home message about experiments that satisfy core assumptions: Any given experiment may overstate or understate the ATE but, over hypothetical replications of the experiment, the average result will recover the ATE.

2.11 EXTRAPOLATION

An experiment's results reflect the specific conditions under which it was conducted: the subjects, the treatment, the context in which the subjects received the treatment, and the outcome measures. Whether we can safely generalize results obtained from these specific conditions to other subjects, treatments, contexts, or outcomes is an open question. The term "external validity" is used to characterize studies whose results hold up when applied to different people or settings.[11]

How could we establish whether a given experimental result generalizes? One approach is to replicate the experiment with a different group of participants, in a different location, under different conditions, and with an assortment of outcome measures. Sometimes researchers conduct the same experiment in multiple sites to assess whether the results hold up under different circumstances. For example, the Moving to Opportunity study gave randomly selected low-income residents of public housing vouchers that enabled them to move to private housing in less poor neighborhoods. Outcomes included family members' employment, health, encounters with law enforcement, and long-term effects on schooling (Chetty et al. 2016). The experiment was conducted in Baltimore, Boston, Chicago, Los Angeles, and New York City during the 1990s. The array of urban sites produced similar results, suggesting that the effects of relocation out of public housing were not specific to each site's housing markets, economic vitality, or school systems.[12] Multisite studies cannot settle the question of external validity, as there will always be subjects and settings that have not been examined, but they do provide some indication of how variable the results are likely to be.

Another complementary approach is to investigate whether treatment effects are notably different across subjects within a given experiment. For example, pilot tests of school interventions sometimes find promising results among children drawn from mixed-income neighborhoods, and the question is whether similar results would hold among low-income communities. In order to shed light on this question, researchers partition their subject pool by family income and assess whether treatment effects among middle-income subjects are similar to treatment effects among low-income subjects. If so, they can be a bit more sanguine about generalizing to low-income sites. One advantage of working with experiments that encompass a diverse collection of subjects and contexts is they allow researchers to explore whether apparent treatment effects generalize.

---

[11] By contrast, the term "internal validity" refers to whether the experiment at hand generates unbiased causal inferences about the average treatment effect given its subjects, treatment, context, and outcome measures. We evaluate internal validity by considering whether all three core assumptions for unbiased inference are satisfied by a given experiment.

[12] For other examples of multisite studies designed to shed light on generalizability across contexts, see Dunning et al. (2019) and Blair and McClendon (2021).

Because extrapolation inevitably involves forecasting outside the range of one's data, researchers must always rely to some extent on theoretical conjectures about why the intervention works and whether the same causal mechanism is likely to operate in a different set of circumstances. These conjectures in effect fill in the data that have yet to be gathered across the many types of subjects, settings, interventions, and outcomes that have yet to be studied. Theoretical conjectures can be valuable when they are correct, but they are also fallible. One reason that scholars are so interested in replications is that they shed light not only on whether an experimental finding generalizes, but also on whether the theoretical conjectures that aid generalization are themselves trustworthy.

2.12 CONCLUSION

This chapter presented key concepts that may be classified into four categories. The first set clarifies what question an experiment aims to answer. What is the treatment? What is the control? What is the outcome? The second set encompasses more general terminology for thinking about causality and the target of inference. The concept of a potential outcome clarifies what we mean by a causal effect for each subject and the average treatment effect across all subjects. Third, thinking about the sampling distribution of an estimator invites us to step back and reflect on the conditions under which our research methods are capable of informing our understanding of cause and effect. Whether you are reading or conducting a study, consider potential threats to core assumptions and ways that they might be addressed through improvements in experimental design. Finally, reflect on whether one can generalize reliably from an existing experimental body of evidence. If not, what further experiments are required?

EXERCISES

2.1 Defining and Implementing the Treatment: Mutz and Reeves (2005) study the effects of exposure to televised "uncivil discourse" by candidates running for office and its effects on viewers' trust in politicians, measured in a survey completed shortly after exposure to treatment. The researchers hired actors to portray political candidates and crafted the shows as follows.

Two versions of each exchange were taped on the talk show set. The candidates expressed exactly the same issue positions in the same words in both versions and offered exactly the same arguments in support of their positions. But in the civil version the candidates went to extremes to be polite to the opposition, inserting phrases such as "I'm really glad Bob raised the issue of ..." and "I don't disagree with all of your points, Bob, but ..." before calmly making their own positions clear. Both candidates fully observed the interpersonal norms for civility in expressing their viewpoints, not only in their own speech, but also by waiting patiently while the other person answered and by paying attention to the opponent while he was speaking.

In the uncivil version of these exchanges, the candidates used the same script but inserted gratuitous asides that suggested a lack of respect for and/or frustration with the opposition. Sample statements include comments such as "You're really missing the point here, Neil" and "What Bob is completely overlooking is . . ." The candidates also raised their voices and never apologized for interrupting one another. Nonverbal cues such as rolling of the eyes and rueful shaking of the head from side to side were also used to suggest lack of respect for what the opponent was saying (pp. 4–5).

Their experiment involves three randomly assigned groups: some participants watch the civil debate; others, the uncivil debate; and a control group does not watch any political content.

a. Explain how the meaning of the average treatment effect changes when we compare civil versus uncivil as opposed to control versus uncivil.

b. What are the advantages and disadvantages of using actors to portray civil or uncivil political candidates, as opposed to footage of actual candidates?

2.2 A study by Rind and Bordia (1996) tested whether restaurant tips increase, on average, when waitstaff write "smiley faces" on the backs of the bills they submit to customers. After the customers finished eating, waitstaff randomly assigned each bill to either receive a smiley face or not. These bills were presented with no further interaction with the customers. The outcome measure was the percentage tip that customers paid on each bill.

a. Who or what are the subjects in this experiment?

b. Why do you suppose that the random assignment was conducted after the customers were finished?

c. Why do you suppose that bills were presented with no further interaction with customers?

d. The researchers used tips as the outcome measure. What are the advantages or disadvantages of using tips instead of administering a survey at the conclusion of each meal?

2.3 Panagopoulos (2011) sent the treatment group mailings that thanked them for voting in a previous election. One control group received no mail. Another group received a letter that reminded them about a coming election but did not reference their past participation. (Examples of the three mailings may be found in the online appendix.)

a. What causal effect does the researcher isolate when comparing the voting rate among those who received the thank-you-for-voting mail to the voting rate among those who received the reminder mail?

b. How is this causal effect different from the effect of receiving the thank-you-for-voting mail versus receiving no mailing?

c. Can this experimental design be used to assess whether the reminder mailing increased turnout? Why or why not?

2.4 In order to assess whether experimental participants discriminate on the basis of race, Iyengar and Westwood (2015) asked participants to compare two otherwise similar high school applicants for a college scholarship. The applicants' races are not stated explicitly on the applications. Instead, one applicant, Jamal Washington, lists that he is "President of the African American Student Association" while the other applicant, Arthur Wolfe, lists that he is "President of the Future Investment Banker Club." If half of the participants give the scholarship to Jamal Washington and half to Arthur Wolfe, does this imply that these participants made their scholarship decisions in a race-blind way? Why or why not?

2.5 How is a potential outcome different from an observed outcome?

2.6 Define the term "average treatment effect."

2.7 What does it mean to say that "random assignment creates treatment and control groups that are identical, in expectation"?

2.8 What is a sampling distribution?

2.9 What is a standard error?

2.10 What does it mean to say that an estimator generates unbiased estimates of the average treatment effect?

2.11 Table 2.1 illustrates an experiment in which the first two subjects are treated and the next three subjects are not treated. Column (2) shows which potential outcomes are revealed by which subjects. The observed mean in the treatment group is 18, while the observed mean in the control group is 24. The difference-in-means estimate is therefore 18 − 24 = −6.

    a. Use the potential outcomes in Table 2.1 to calculate the difference-in-means estimate if Subjects #1 and 3 had been assigned to treatment while the remaining three subjects were assigned to control.

    b. Referring to Table 2.1, the text shows the 10 possible random assignments that place exactly two subjects into treatment and three subjects into control. These random assignments produce an array of different estimates of the ATE; however, the average of these estimates is exactly equal to the ATE. Now imagine a different experimental design places just one subject into treatment and the other four into control. Show that the five possible random assignments produce estimates that, on average, equal the true ATE.

    c. Which has a larger standard error, the design in which exactly two of five subjects are placed into treatment or the design in which exactly one of five subjects is placed into treatment?

2.12 What are the three core assumptions for unbiased inference?

2.13 Select any published study that purports to show a causal relationship between some kind of intervention and an outcome.

    a. Explain what each core assumption means in the context of this study.

    b. Which core assumptions seem most or least defensible in this study?

2.14 What is the scientific value of replicating an experiment that was conducted in the past using the same procedures but a different set of participants?

APPENDIX 2.1: PROOF THAT DIFFERENCE-IN-MEANS AND DIFFERENCES-IN-CHANGE SCORES PRODUCE UNBIASED ESTIMATES OF THE AVERAGE TREATMENT EFFECT

A formal proof of this proposition may be found in Gerber and Green (2012, p. 35). The proof offered here attempts to make the same point without algebra.

Suppose we list the N subjects in our study in a random order. Call the first m subjects on this list the treatment group and the next $N - m$ subjects the control group. Because the treatment group is a random sample of all N subjects, their average treated potential outcomes are expected to be the same as the average treated potential outcomes for all N subjects. *Expected* here refers to the average outcome we would obtain from all possible random assignments. Similarly, because the control group is a random sample of all N subjects, their average untreated potential outcomes are expected to be the same as the average untreated potential outcomes for all N subjects. The difference-in-means estimator is the difference between the average observed outcome in the treatment group and the average observed outcome in the control group. By substituting the expected outcomes for the actual outcomes, we obtain the ATE, which completes the proof.

The proof for change scores works in a similar way. Because the covariate is unaffected by treatment assignment (recall that covariates are measured prior to treatment assignment), the same covariate value is subtracted from a subject's observed outcome regardless of whether the subject is treated or not. Because the same constant is subtracted from both treated and untreated outcomes, the covariate has no expected effect on the difference between the average change score in the treatment group and the average change score in the control group. Over all possible random assignments, the difference-in-change-score estimator will on average recover the ATE.

3

Conducting a Practice Experiment
(Not Involving Human Subjects)

The purpose of this chapter is to give readers a feel for how experiments are designed, implemented, and analyzed. The chapter walks through the steps of designing a small, inexpensive experiment that can be conducted at home. We will also discuss the fine points of implementing an experiment, assembling a dataset, and preparing a statistical analysis. In order to put aside ethical issues that apply to experiments involving human participants, this chapter confines its attention to product testing. Drawing inspiration from the first field experiments conducted a century ago, my running example will test the effects of fertilizer on plant growth (Fisher 1926).[1] I will walk through my reasoning as I design the experiment to help you design your own experiment. Later in the chapter, I describe some illustrative experiments conducted by students on topics such as cooking, the preservation of carved pumpkins, and evoking video recommendations from YouTube. These students have generously provided their data, planning documents, and R code so that you can retrace their steps.

3.1 POSING A TESTABLE EXPERIMENTAL QUESTION

Think about comparing two states of the world, one that involves some kind of intervention and the other without it. How different would the outcomes be, on average, with or without the intervention?

Start by posing a research question that a randomized experiment can answer. For example, one could ask, "How much larger do plants grow on average when this fertilizer and water solution is applied instead of an equivalent amount of water alone?" Framing the question in this way sets up a comparison between treatment (fertilizer plus water) versus control (just water).

What kinds of questions are not well suited to randomized experimentation? One category includes questions that focus solely on describing outcomes, with no comparison of treatment and control. For example, the question, "How often do plants die after receiving the recommended dose of fertilizer?" involves no control group. It focuses

---

[1] Fisher went on to revolutionize the design and analysis of randomized trials.

solely on describing outcomes in the treatment group. To make it more amenable to the kind of experimental designs described in this book, rephrase the question to ask how the death rate in the wake of treatment compares to the death rate after some other intervention, such as applications of water without fertilizer.

3.2 ASSEMBLING TREATMENTS AND SUBJECTS

What is the treatment? The particular brand of plant fertilizer whose effects I will be testing comes in a liquid concentrate that, according to the instructions on the label, must be diluted with water at a specified ratio and applied twice, first when the plant is initially transplanted and again a week later. Although I am not obligated to follow these instructions, it seems sensible to do so since the manufacturer has a commercial incentive to give instructions that make its product perform well.

What does the control condition consist of? This question requires a bit of thought because what the control group receives will profoundly shape how we will interpret the results. Carefully consider whether the control group should receive some alternative intervention or nothing at all. In the case of fertilizer that is applied with water, one option is to compare the fertilizer-plus-water treatment to water alone, which isolates the specific effect of fertilizer. Suppose, instead, I were to give nothing to the control group at the time of treatment. That design would enable me to assess the effects of applying the fertilizer and water mixture as opposed to doing nothing, which might simulate an intervention set in motion by a gardener who chances upon fertilizer concentrate in a store but who otherwise would have taken no action. This design answers a meaningful question even if it would not allow us to separate the effects of fertilizer from the effects of watering. Another possible line of testing would be to compare this particular brand of fertilizer to a different brand of fertilizer. That design makes sense when the causal question comes down to which fertilizer product works best. Acknowledging that several different designs have merit, I will opt for the first design, because I most want to know whether it pays to add fertilizer if I am already watering my plants.

Having settled on the treatment and control conditions, I must next select my experimental subjects. In principle, one could apply fertilizer to any species of plant, but what kinds of plants are presumed to be relevant? I could have grown flowers or vegetables, but I happen to be interested in whether fertilizer helps birch tree seedlings, since that is what I transplant every year in order to reforest a patch of barren land near my home. I could not determine whether this product purports to accelerate the growth of tree seedlings, so I will be careful to temper my conclusions. Even if the fertilizer does not work for tree seedlings, it could still work for other types of plants.[2]

---

[2] This experiment also involved other species of trees, such as maples and dogwoods. I focus here on birches for ease of presentation. I obtain similar results using other tree species, both in this experiment and in subsequent tests. See the exercises in the online *R Companion* for an example.

3.3 DEFINING AND MEASURING OUTCOMES

What kinds of observable effects might the treatment have? In the case of plant fertilizer, the central claim is that treated plants will grow faster than they would otherwise. I will therefore need to measure the size of each plant at the end of the study. Perhaps I could unearth each plant and weigh it? That seems messy and could harm the plants. I settled instead on a less demanding option: Measure each plant's height above the soil line. Intuition suggests that a seedling's height is a valid indicator of its vitality. To prevent bias from creeping into the measurements, I asked a family member, who was blind to the hypothesis and treatment assignments, to measure each plant's height.

I could have gone much further in my assessment of plant vitality. For example, I could have also counted the total number of leaves on each plant. Another option would have been to inspect the color and robustness of each plant, rating its vitality on a scale from 0 to 10. Such an assessment is somewhat subjective, although one could imagine obtaining a consensus opinion from trained horticulturists. If you decide to gather observers' ratings, consider photographing each plant to help systematize the rating process and make it reproducible. And, as always, blind the raters to the treatment condition of each plant so that their judgments will not be affected by their expectations about the treatment's effect.

In addition to deciding what to measure, you must also decide when outcomes will be assessed. How long will the experiment last? Does the manufacturer indicate when the product's effects will become apparent? If you are uncertain, feel free to measure outcomes at more than one point in time, for example, three and six weeks after treatment. Although this approach requires extra effort, it can provide useful insights into how treatment effects unfold over time. It may be, for example, that the "Quick Start" that this fertilizer product provides subsides over time, and plants in the control group eventually catch up to the treatment group.

3.4 CONTEXT

Where will the experiment take place and under what conditions? If the experiment is to take place outdoors, take note of circumstances that might help readers think about the generalizability of your results to other contexts. For example, what was the average temperature? How much rainfall occurred over the course of the study? Were plants positioned in the shade or in full sun? Again, photographs make it easier to convey the context to interested readers.

My study was conducted in the Hudson Valley during midsummer, with temperatures averaging 85°F. During this sunny dry spell, I watered the plants every morning. This particular detail is important. Suppose that I had not watered at all, causing all the plants to wilt and die. That would have made the fertilizer treatment look ineffective, but this conclusion would have been misleading since this product presupposes that the plants receive basic care. Conducting a fair test means disclosing key details that enable readers to draw informed conclusions from the results.

Even if your experiment takes place indoors or under controlled conditions, it is nevertheless important to be attentive to the physical arrangement. Rather than plant the seedlings in a bed of soil, I planted them in separate pots. In a bed of soil, fertilizer applied to one plant could affect neighboring plants, thereby jeopardizing the *noninterference assumption*. If fertilizer had seeped into the control group plants, all of the plants would have been treated, and we might have mistakenly concluded that the fertilizer was ineffective because outcomes in the treatment and control groups were similar. I was also careful not to introduce procedures that might jeopardize the *symmetry assumption*, which presumes that the treatment is the only factor that differs systematically between the treatment and control conditions. For example, in order to make it easy to apply the treatment and measure outcomes, I was tempted to place the treatment plants in one location and the control plants in another location. But doing so risks exposing one of the experimental groups to more sunlight, which means that we will not be able to distinguish the effects of the treatment from the effects of sunlight. To avoid this problem, I placed my seedlings in the order in which they were potted, since that is unrelated to their assigned treatment.

3.5 COMPILING A DATASET

Careful documentation is crucial to the success of any experimental project. Begin by creating the computer files that store the data, generate the random assignments, and include notes about what was done, when, and why. Opensource software such as R makes data analysis free, and the Open Science Framework repository is a free resource for storing your data, code, and research materials. For introductory guides to R and Open Science Framework, see the online appendix and *R Companion*.

The process of building a dataset begins by creating an identifier for each subject. This identifier could be a name or identification number. For example, here is the R code for labeling the 12 plants in my study:

```
# add labels
labels <- c("Plant1", "Plant2", "Plant3", "Plant4", "Plant5",
            "Plant6", "Plant7", "Plant8", "Plant9", "Plant10",
            "Plant11", "Plant12")
```

Before launching the study, measure covariates (i.e., background attributes of the subjects) that might later predict outcomes. In this example, the outcome is each plant's height measured three weeks after fertilizer was applied. Height *prior* to random assignment is likely to be a strong predictor of height at the conclusion of the study. If we record prior height, we can later calculate how much the height of each seedling *changed* over the course of the experiment. For the reasons described in Chapter 2, change scores often provide more insight into the effectiveness of a treatment than raw scores gathered at the end of the experiment.

Here are the heights (in inches) prior to random assignment:

```
pre_height <- c(16, 17, 24, 21, 27, 30, 19, 28, 27, 19, 24, 17)
```

With these basic features of the dataset in place, I randomly assigned these 12 subjects such that exactly six are assigned to the treatment condition and six are assigned to the control condition. The R package `randomizr` makes this assignment easy:

```
install.packages("randomizr")    # install the randomizr package
library(randomizr)               # load randomizr library of functions
treat <- complete_ra(N=12,m=6)   # complete assignment: N=12 subjects, m=6 in treatment
```

Using the `cbind()` function, I displayed the labels, baseline height, and treatment assignments side-by-side to verify that I inputted the results correctly:

```
cbind(labels,treat,pre_height)   # show the data as randomized
```

I brought this handy list of treatment assignments to the site of my experiment. To keep track of which plants were to receive treatment, I identified each plant by affixing a large label to its pot. I gave each plant in the treatment group the recommended dosage of fertilizer-plus-water mixture and gave an equivalent amount of water (only) to plants assigned to the control group. In order to document the process, I took photos with my smartphone.

After administering the treatment, I next arranged the plants for the duration of the experiment. To avoid accidentally exposing one of the experimental groups to more moisture or sunlight, I arranged them according to their plant ID number, since the assigned treatment is statistically independent of these ID numbers. From this point on, I did everything possible to preserve the symmetry assumption by treating all plants in the same manner. For example, I ignored treatment assignments when watering or weeding. In hindsight, I should have spaced the plants a bit farther apart from one another, in case the treatment of one plant had repercussions for the growth of an adjacent plant. For example, if fertilizer had caused the treated plants to grow rapidly and shade their control group counterparts, the noninterference assumption would have been jeopardized.

3.6 PAUSE TO WRITE A PLANNING DOCUMENT

Once the experimental design becomes clear, but before you measure outcomes, describe it in a *planning document* so that you don't forget the details. Create a document known as a *pre-analysis plan* – which can be prose or just annotated lines of R code – that describes the analysis that you plan to conduct once outcomes have been gathered. Following a plan conceived before the results are known helps reassure readers that your statistical analysis is honest and objective. In the absence of a plan, researchers may be tempted to riffle through different ways of analyzing the data before settling on one that supports some preconceived conclusion. Posting the planning document with a date stamp assures the reader that the plan was developed before outcomes were obtained. Open Science Framework makes it easy to create public-facing pre-analysis plans. Instructions and examples may be found in the online appendix.

3.7 MEASURING OUTCOMES

Three weeks later, I was ready to measure the height of each plant. I asked a family member who was blind to the treatment assignments to do it for me (my role was to assist the measurement process by carrying pots to a measurement station). To record the results, I created an outcome variable, `post_height`, with entries for each of the observations.

Scatterplot

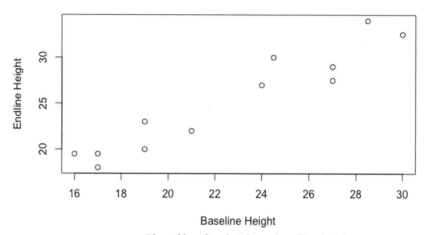

FIGURE 3.1. Plot of baseline height and endline height

```
post_height <- c(20, 20, 27, 22, 28, 32, 23, 34, 29, 20, 30, 18)
```

The next line of code displays the updated dataset, which now includes this outcome:

```
> cbind(labels,treat,pre_height,post_height) # updated dataset with outcomes
```

Once you have gathered outcomes, you are close to the fun part of the study – learning from the experimental results. But before you rush to find out whether the treatment worked, take a few moments to inspect the data for coding errors or other anomalies. Sorting these problems out now may save you a good deal of grief later.

Inspecting the data involves checking your records to make sure that you did not make an error transcribing numbers, perhaps accidentally putting outcomes for subject #3 where you meant to record outcomes for subject #4. Graphs are another helpful way to inspect the data for coding errors. I plotted pre_height and post_height as shown in Figure 3.1 in order to see whether any of the points look misplaced:

```
plot(pre_height,post_height, main="Scatterplot",xlab="Baseline Height", ylab="Endline Height")
```

Baseline height is a strong predictor of endline height. The points on the graph shown in Figure 3.1 drift from the lower left corner (relatively short at baseline and endline) to the upper right corner (relatively tall at baseline and endline).

3.8 CHECKING COVARIATE BALANCE

When you are satisfied that the data have been entered correctly, verify that random assignment created groups that have similar background profiles. In my experiment, the background variable of interest is pre_height. The distribution of baseline heights in the treatment group should be similar to that in the control group. I plotted the data to visually inspect the degree of similarity. Figure 3.2 adds some random "jitter" to the

Scatterplot

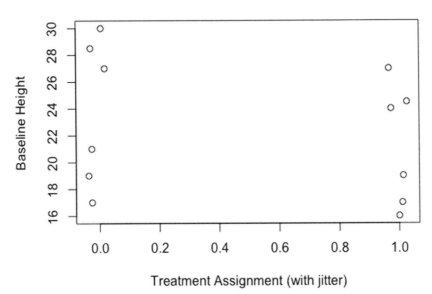

FIGURE 3.2. Plot of treatment assignment and baseline height

treat variable so that all points will be visible, even if two observations happen to have the same (X, Y) coordinates. Instead of plotting treat on the horizontal axis, we plot treat plus a random normal number using the syntax rnorm(12,mean=0,sd=.03):

```
plot(treat+rnorm(12, mean=0, sd=.03), pre_height, main="Scatterplot", xlab="Treatment Assignment
    (with jitter)", ylab="Baseline Height")
```

The averages depicted in Figure 3.2 seem similar in the two groups, perhaps a shade lower in the treatment group. I obtain more specific information by calculating the means for each group:

```
> mean(pre_height[ treat==0] )
[1]  23.75
> mean(pre_height[ treat==1] )
[1]  21.25
```

It appears that the treatment group started at a slight disadvantage, insofar as its baseline heights were on average 2.5 inches shorter.

3.9 ESTIMATING THE AVERAGE TREATMENT EFFECT

With preliminaries out of the way, it is time to see if the treatment worked as expected. Examine the distribution of outcomes by experimental condition in order to get a feel for whether the intervention caused the distribution of outcomes in the treatment group to look different from the distribution of outcomes in the control group. Figure 3.3 graphs post_height for the treatment and control groups (with horizontal jitter added so that all points are visible):

Outcomes by Experimental Group

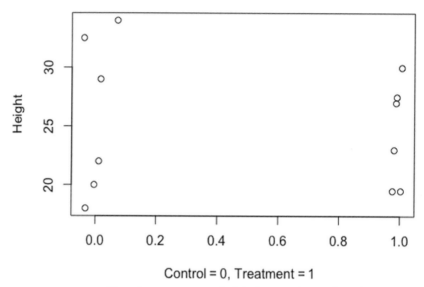

Control = 0, Treatment = 1

FIGURE 3.3. Plot of post-treatment height by experimental condition

```
plot(treat+rnorm(12, mean=0, sd=.03), post_height, main="Outcomes by Experimental Group",
xlab="Control=0, Treatment=1", ylab="Height")
```

Displaying the data in this way gives a sense of whether the treatment group's average outcome (on the vertical axis) is noticeably higher or lower than the control group's average. In this case, the two groups seem to have similar averages.

Having gotten an initial impression of how outcomes in the treatment and control group compare, I estimate the average effect of the treatment by comparing the average outcome in the control group to the average outcome in the treatment group:

```
> mean(post_height[ treat==0] )
[ 1]  25.91667
> mean(post_height[ treat==1] )
[ 1]  24.41667
```

In this case, the treatment group average is 24.4 inches, and the control group average is 25.9 inches. The difference is therefore −1.5, implying that birch seedlings assigned to fertilizer were, on average, 1.5 inches *shorter* than their control group counterparts three weeks after treatment. I found this estimate surprising. How much faith should I place in this result?

3.10 ASSESSING STATISTICAL UNCERTAINTY

Our experiment generated an unexpected result – the fertilizer seemed to stunt the growth of the birch seedlings. Before concluding that fertilizer is worse than useless, we must remember that our estimate of −1.5 inches reflects a single random assignment of subjects to treatment and control groups. If this experiment were repeated under the same conditions but with a different random assignment, the apparent difference between the new treatment and control groups would likely change.

The collection of estimates from all possible random assignments of subjects to treatment or control is known as the *sampling distribution*. The more dispersed the sampling distribution, the less we learn from the experimental results. Recall from Chapter 2 that the conventional way to characterize the dispersion of the sampling distribution is in terms of the *standard error*, which is the standard deviation of the sampling distribution. The larger the standard error, the more the estimated average treatment effect varies from one random assignment to the next. In addition to estimating the average treatment effect, it is also instructive to estimate its standard error.

The formula for estimating the standard error requires us to first calculate the standard deviation in the control group and the standard deviation in the treatment group.

```
sd_control        <- sd(post_height[ treat==0] )
sd_treatment      <- sd(post_height[ treat==1] )
```

We also calculate the number of observations in the control and treatment groups, as these quantities will be used later.

```
n_control         <- length(post_height[ treat==0] )
n_treatment       <- length(post_height[ treat==1] )
```

Let's also assign names to the mean outcomes in control and treatment, so that we can include them when we summarize the results.

```
mean_control      <- mean(post_height[ treat==0] )
mean_treatment    <- mean(post_height[ treat==1] )
```

```
cbind(n_control,n_treatment,mean_treatment,mean_control, sd_treatment,sd_control)
    n_control n_treatment mean_treatment mean_control sd_treatment sd_control
[1,]        6           6      24.41667     25.91667     4.420596   6.800123
```

The standard deviation in the treatment group is found to be 4.4, and the standard deviation in the control group is found to be 6.8. To estimate the standard error for the difference-in-means estimator of the average treatment effect, we use the formula:

$$\widehat{Standard}\ Error = \sqrt{\frac{Standard\ Deviation^2_{control}}{N_{control}} + \frac{Standard\ Deviation^2_{treatment}}{N_{treatment}}} \tag{3.1}$$

Implementing this formula in R yields a standard error of 3.31.

```
difference_in_means <- mean_treatment - mean_control
standard_error <- sqrt(sd_control^2/n_control + sd_treatment^2/n_treatment)
cbind(difference_in_means, standard_error)
```

```
     difference_in_means standard_error
[1,]                -1.5       3.311176
```

What does the standard error of 3.31 tell us? The larger the standard error, the farther our estimate of −1.5 may be from the true, unknown average treatment effect. Our best guess is −1.5, but we would like to make a statement of the form, "The following interval has a 95% chance of bracketing the true average treatment effect." The term "95% confidence interval" is shorthand for intervals that have this property.[3] These intervals are calculated based on the assumption that the sampling distribution looks like a *t*-distribution (a bell-shaped curve with somewhat fatter tails). In small studies (like this one), the sampling distribution will follow a *t*-distribution when outcomes are normally distributed in both the treatment and control groups. In large studies (with more than 60 subjects in each experimental group, the requirements are more forgiving so long as the distributions of outcomes in treatment and control are not terribly lopsided (Sawilowsky and Blair 1992).[4]

Using a *t*-distribution to form a 95% confidence interval requires three steps. The first step is to calculate the effective number of observations, or *degrees of freedom*. In this case N = 12 and we consume one degree of freedom to estimate the treatment group mean and another to estimate the control group mean, so the remaining degrees of freedom are N − 2 = 10. Next, we calculate the lower side of the confidence interval. To calculate how many standard errors below the estimated ATE we need to travel in the *t*-distribution, we use the R syntax: qt(.025,10, lower.tail= FALSE), which returns 2.228139. That tells us we need to travel 2.23 standard errors below the estimate (−1.5) to reach the lower interval. That gives us a lower interval of −1.5 − (2.23)(3.31) = −8.9. The final step is to estimate the upper interval. This time we add 2.23-times the standard error to our estimate to obtain −1.5 + (2.23)(3.31) = 5.9.

Using R, the calculation looks as follows:

```
t_multiplier <- qt(.025, 10, lower.tail= FALSE)

lower_interval <- difference_in_means - t_multiplier* standard_error
upper_interval <- difference_in_means + t_multiplier* standard_error

cbind(lower_interval, upper_interval)

     lower_interval upper_interval
[1,]      -8.877761       5.877761
```

In other words, the interval ranging from −8.9 to 5.9 has a 95 percent chance of bracketing the average treatment effect. The width of this interval suggests that our estimate is subject to a good deal of uncertainty. Our estimated ATE indicates that the treatment reduced growth by 1.5 inches. However, it is possible that this fertilizer truly increases growth by a few inches but by chance we drew an estimate of −1.5 from the sampling distribution.

---

[3] Confidence intervals will vary from one random assignment to the next if we were to replicate the study under identical conditions. Across all possible random assignments, 95 percent of the intervals formed in this way will bracket the true average treatment effect.

[4] An example of a lopsided, or skewed, distribution of outcomes is campaign donations. Experiments that attempt to promote donations typically find that most of the treatment group contributes nothing, but a few people contribute large sums. A *t*-distribution tends to do a poor job of characterizing the sampling distribution in this case (see Schwam-Baird et al. 2016, for an example). We revisit the *t*-distribution in Chapter 7 (see Box 7.3).

3.11 USING CHANGE SCORES TO GET MORE PRECISE ESTIMATES OF THE ATE

Researchers often wonder how they can obtain more precise estimates, that is, estimates with smaller standard errors and narrower confidence intervals. One way is to conduct experiments with more subjects. Intuition suggests that if each experimental group contained a very large number of subjects, the average outcomes in each experimental group will change very little from one randomization to the next. In my experiment, I could have assembled more birch seedlings and assigned them to treatment and control. Because the standard error declines with the square root of the number of subjects, quadrupling the number of plants would, all else being equal, cut the standard errors in half.

Another way to improve precision is to reduce the variability of the outcome measure by working with subjects that are initially as similar as possible. For example, my collection of seedlings could have been restricted so that initially all of the plants were the same height. Lacking a sufficient number of similar size birches, I was unable to use this tactic.

An alternative approach is to make the current collection of 12 birches more similar to each other by using the covariate, the baseline height of each plant. Instead of defining the outcome as each plant's height after three weeks, define the outcome as the *change* in height over the span of three weeks. Using R, we define `change_height` as the difference between post_height and pre_height:

```
change_height <- post_height - pre_height
```

Comparing the new dependent variable, `change_height`, to `post_height`, we see that change scores have a much smaller standard deviation. That means that the numerators in Eq. (3.1) are smaller, implying that the estimated standard error will shrink when we use this outcome. Using the same R code but swapping `change_height` for `post_height`, we calculate means and standard deviations:

```
mean_control <- mean(change_height[ treat==0] )
mean_treatment   <- mean(change_height[ treat==1] )

sd_control   <- sd(change_height[ treat==0] )
sd_treatment <- sd(change_height[ treat==1] )

cbind(n_control, n_treatment, mean_treatment, mean_control, sd_treatment, sd_control)
     n_control n_treatment mean_treatment mean_control sd_treatment sd_control
[ 1,]        6           6       3.166667     2.166667      1.66333    1.75119
```

Next, we calculate the difference-in-means and the standard error:

```
difference_in_means <- mean_treatment - mean_control
standard_error <- sqrt(sd_control^2/n_control + sd_treatment^2/n_treatment)

cbind(difference_in_means,standard_error)

      difference_in_means standard_error
[ 1,]                   1      0.9860133
```

My revised estimate of the average treatment effect is now 1 rather than −1.5. I take this revised estimate to be more credible because its estimated standard error is smaller, 0.99. That standard error is roughly one-third as large as the standard error of 3.31 we obtained when analyzing `post_height`. As you will see from the exercises at the end of the chapter, the 95% confidence interval is now much narrower, which is another sign that working with change scores has reduced our uncertainty.

3.12 DRAWING BOTH SUBSTANTIVE AND STATISTICAL CONCLUSIONS

What do I conclude from my experimental results? With just 12 observations, my experiment does not give a precise indication of whether fertilizer promotes growth. My best guess, based on an analysis of change scores, is that this fertilizer increases plant height by an inch over the course of three weeks. Is that a lot or a little? I am not sure that I would go to the trouble of buying and applying this product for an extra inch of seedling height.

That said, the confidence interval remains wide, which means that a larger study might generate more favorable results. One virtue of conducting a small study such as this one is that I now have a better sense of how much data I need to collect in the future if I redo this study. Since the standard error declines with the square root of N, conducting an experiment with 48 observations instead of 12 should reduce the standard error by a factor of 2, to just half an inch. This experiment did not settle the research question that we posed, but we now have a clearer understanding of what effect sizes are plausible and what kind of study is needed to pin down the answer with precision.

3.13 ILLUSTRATIVE EXPERIMENTS CONDUCTED BY STUDENTS

In order to spark your imagination as you consider experiments that you might conduct on your own, I have selected a few thought-provoking examples of student-run experiments that do not involve human subjects. I will briefly summarize each one, calling attention to noteworthy design features. The authors have graciously shared their planning documents, data, and write-ups so that you can retrace their steps.

Does Hairspray Preserve Pumpkins? Inspired by blog posts recommending the use of hairspray to preserve carved pumpkins,[5] Marnie Ginis conducted a randomized experiment on 30 small pumpkins.[6] Prior to the launch of the experiment, each pumpkin's "height was measured in centimeters from the bottom to the highest point of the pumpkin (not including stem)." The 15 pumpkins assigned to treatment "had their interior coated with hairspray immediately after being carved," while "pumpkins in control were carved but not coated with hairspray." After the treatment was administered, pumpkins were arranged in random locations in a 3-by-10 grid indoors near a window. They were left for two weeks, at which point each pumpkin's height was measured again. The outcome is the change in height between the initial measurement

---

[5] https://cafemom.com/lifestyle/177708-preserve_halloween_carved_pumpkin_rotting/120377-bleach_
solution
[6] Marnie Ginis, *Practicum Experiment*, November 17, 2020.

Box 3.1 Checklist of Items to Discuss When Summarizing Your Experiment

1. Theory
    a. Background or motivation: What puzzle or unanswered question inspired the current study?
    b. Hypothesis: What causal claim does your experiment address? Are you expecting the intervention to increase the outcome, decrease the outcome, or change the outcome in some unspecified direction?
2. Design
    a. Intervention: What is the treatment? What is the control condition to which the treatment will be compared?
    b. Subjects: Who or what are the experimental subjects?
    c. Random assignment: How are subjects allocated to treatment and control conditions? How many subjects are assigned to each condition?
    d. Covariate balance check: Do treatment and control groups have similar background attributes, as expected under random assignment?
    e. Setting: In what context are the subjects exposed to the treatment (or placebo)?
    f. Outcomes: How are outcomes measured? Were you able to obtain outcome measures for all subjects? If not, are the rates of attrition similar in the treatment and control groups?
3. Results
    a. What are the average outcomes in treatment and control? What are the standard deviations in treatment and control?
    b. Estimate the average treatment effect, its standard error, and the 95% confidence interval. Interpret these results.
4. Conclusions
    a. What did you learn about the treatment's average effect?
    b. What are the next steps in this line of research?

---

and the post-treatment measurement two weeks later. The hypothesis is that hairspray slows the rate of pumpkin collapse, implying that, on average, treated pumpkins will shrink less than their control group counterparts.

Table 3.1 provides equivocal support for the hypothesis. Yes, pumpkins coated with hairspray on average experienced less shrinkage than pumpkins in the control group, but the difference is small, just one-quarter of a centimeter. The standard error of this estimated effect is also one-quarter of a centimeter. Can you form a 95% confidence interval?[7] If the top of this interval were the true effect, would the effect be large enough to be consequential?

Do Your Viewing Choices Affect What Political Videos YouTube Recommends? Many political commentators worry that online media contributes to ideological

---

[7] Hint: Since there are $30 - 2 = 28$ degrees of freedom, use the syntax qt(.025, 28, lower.tail= FALSE) to find the number of standard errors you need to travel from the estimate to reach the top or bottom of the interval. The standard error is given in Table 3.1.

TABLE 3.1. *Shrinkage (in centimeters) of pumpkin height over two weeks, by assigned treatment*

	Control	Treatment	Estimated Average Treatment Effect
Mean	1.61 cm	1.36 cm	−0.25 cm
Standard Deviation	0.94	0.58	
Standard Error			0.28
N	15	15	

TABLE 3.2. *Number of conservative video recommendations, by assigned treatment*

	Control	Treatment (Hannity)	Estimated Average Treatment Effect
Mean	0.13	1.33	1.20
Standard Deviation	0.35	0.98	
Standard Error			0.27
N	15	15	

polarization. One concern is that those who choose to view a conservative (liberal) program on a platform such as YouTube will find that the recommendations for subsequent viewing will include more programs of conservative (liberal) valance. Shortly after the 2020 US election, Bardia Rahmani set out to test the extent to which YouTube's recommendations were influenced by a single viewing of a conservative video, in this case a Fox News video entitled "Hannity: 70% of Republicans don't believe this election was free, fair – and for good reason!"[8]

The researcher created 30 fresh user accounts for the purpose of the study. Each account visited YouTube at assigned points in time and watched the Hannity video. The 15 treatment visits were made with "YouTube's search and watch algorithms ... enabled"; these algorithms were disabled for the visits by the user accounts in the control group. Outcomes were measured as follows: "After watching the entirety of the video, the researcher navigated to the user's homepage and refreshed the homepage once. The outcome was then recorded. The outcome of interest ... is ... the number of conservative political video recommendations that appear on each user's homepage." This number was scored by another person who was blind to the treatment assignment. In order to prevent the search and watch algorithm from being influenced by other user accounts' visits (a potential threat to the noninterference assumption), the researcher used a virtual private network so that every user would have a different IP address.

Table 3.2 shows the results of this experiment. The average number of conservative video recommendations was just 0.13 in the control group but 1.33 in the treatment group. The estimated average treatment effect is therefore 1.2 with a standard error of 0.27. The confidence interval ranges from 0.65 to 1.75, suggesting that viewing a conservative video clearly increases the number of conservative recommendations.

---

[8] Bardia Rahmani, *Practicum Experiment*, November 2020.

TABLE 3.3. *Poori ratings, by assigned treatment*

	Control (Low Heat)	Treatment (High Heat)	Estimated Average Treatment Effect
Mean	8.53	11.0	2.47
Standard Deviation	1.81	2.24	
Standard Error			0.74
N	15	15	

Even the low end of the confidence interval represents a 400 percent increase in the average number of such recommendations.

Do Pooris Taste Better When Fried at Hotter Temperatures? Pooris are a "a special kind of Indian bread, typically prepared during festivals and celebratory occasions." But controversy surrounds the question of how they are best prepared: "Popular Indian food websites and forums advocate frying pooris at about 350–375°F, while traditional wisdom recommends that the temperature should be greater than 450°F." Monika Yadav brought scientific rigor to this debate by randomly assigning the temperature at which pooris are fried.[9]

The researcher kneaded poori dough and formed 30 circles for frying. The dough circles, the subjects of this experiment, were randomly assigned to either a low-temperature frying pan (350–375°F) or a high-temperature frying pan (475–495°F). The temperatures of the two pans were monitored using a digital laser temperature gun. One treatment and one control poori circle were fried in adjacent pans at the same time. Addressing concerns about the symmetry assumption, the researcher took care to "alternate the heating temperature once for both pans during the course of the experiment to make sure the pan is not, in any way, correlated with treatment assignment." Outcomes were measured by a taste-tester who was blind to treatment condition. Each poori was rated on a series of one to five scales assessing its taste, oil absorption, and puffiness. The researcher's statistical analysis focuses on the sum of the three ratings, a score that ranges from 3 to 15.

The results in Table 3.3 indicate that extra frying heat led to improved ratings. The average rating was 2.47 points greater in the treatment group, which represents more than a one standard deviation increase over the average rating in the control group. The 95% confidence interval extends from 0.95 to 3.99. The precision with which the ATE is estimated makes the demonstrated benefits of extra frying heat quite convincing.

Do Exhausted Batteries Bounce Higher? Myth or fact: Depleted batteries bounce higher than fresh batteries? Kylan Rutherford set out to get to the bottom of this question by conducting a randomized trial involving 30 Amazonbasics AA batteries.[10] Fifteen batteries were randomly assigned to be placed in flashlights for five hours, draining their electric charge. All batteries were then dropped through a 21-inch tube onto a

---

[9] Monika Yadav, *Practicum Experiment – Analysis*, November 22, 2020.
[10] Kylan Rutherford, *Experiment Practicum*.

TABLE 3.4. *Battery bounce times (in seconds), by assigned treatment*

	Control (Fully Charged)	Treatment (Depleted)	Estimated Average Treatment Effect
Mean	0.102	0.227	0.125
Standard Deviation	0.033	0.044	
Standard Error			0.014
N	15	15	

Notes: This table reports results from the first bounce measurement after treatment. The exercises to this chapter examine the average of three post-treatment measurements. The researcher also measured bounce time prior to treatment and, as expected, found average bounce times to be similar in treatment and control.

table. Bounce was measured using a "voice memos app" that digitally recorded the time between the first contact with the table and the second contact. Although this digital recording is accurate to within 0.02 seconds, the researcher repeated the measurements three times to minimize inadvertent variations in the way the battery was dropped down the tube. Thus, there are two versions of the outcome measure: bounce time when measured on the first round and average bounce time across three measurements.

The results from the first bounce test are presented in Table 3.4. The treated batteries bounce for an average of 0.23 seconds, as opposed to 0.10 seconds in the control group. Although a difference of 0.125 seconds is difficult to perceive with the naked ear, the care with which this experiment was executed leaves little doubt that the effect is greater than zero. The standard error is just 0.014 seconds, implying that the confidence interval of the ATE extends from 0.095 to 0.154. Depleted batteries do bounce higher, but the effect may too subtle to be of much practical use.

EXERCISES

The datasets used in the exercises are available from the book's webpage: https://osf.io/b78je/, or you may import them directly into R by installing the package `experimentr`.

3.1 Using the numbers reported in Table 3.1, explain how the standard error was calculated. Calculate the 95% confidence interval for the ATE.

3.2 Use the poori dataset to answer the following questions.
   a. Calculate the means in the treatment group and the control group.
   b. Calculate the standard deviations of outcomes in the treatment group and the control group.
   c. Estimate the average treatment effect.
   d. Estimate the standard error of the average treatment effect you estimated in part (c).
   e. What would you expect the standard error to be if you were to repeat the study but with 60 poori dough balls in treatment and 30 in control?

3.3 Using the `youtube` dataset, plot outcomes by treatment assignment, using horizontal jitter to make all the points visible.

3.4 Using the `batteries` dataset, answer the following questions.

    a. Estimate the average treatment effect and its standard error using the first measurement of bounced height, as the author did.

    b. Repeat these calculations, this time using the average of all three measurements of bounce height.

    c. How does the standard error of the three-measurement average compare to the standard error using just the first measurement? Looking at Eq. (3.1), why would repeated measurement of the outcome change the estimated standard error?

    d. Notice that the author did not use the pretest at all in his analysis; the analysis of the first outcome measurement was based on the post-treatment bounce time, not the change in bounce time from pretest to posttest. Use a graph to show that pretest bounce time is not predictive of posttest bounce time.

    e. Show that the precision with which the ATE is estimated does not seem to improve when one analyzes change scores (first bounce time minus pretest bounce time) instead of the first bounce time only.

3.5 Thinking back to the running example of fertilizer and plant growth, suppose that on the final day of the experiment, a deer wandered into the garden and ate several of the plants.

    a. Would you still measure the outcome (height) for the damaged plants, or would you exclude them from the final round of data collection and measure outcomes only for the undamaged plants? Explain your reasoning.

    b. Some researchers might suggest that you discard the experiment altogether due to the deer grazing incident and try again with a fresh set of plants. Do you agree or disagree with this suggestion, and why?

APPENDIX 3.1: TESTING THE NULL HYPOTHESIS WHEN CHECKING COVARIATE BALANCE

The process of randomly assigning subjects to treatment or control (or to several treatment conditions) may be jeopardized by human error, attrition, or tampering. Even highly professionalized studies have sometimes found that their randomization procedures were not implemented properly. For this reason, it is useful to check whether the covariate profile of the treatment group is similar to the covariate profile in the control group. In this chapter, we did so informally by inspecting the averages in both groups to see if they were similar.

A more rigorous test involves a bit of statistical analysis. We calculate the difference-in-means for a covariate (e.g., a pretest score) by subtracting the covariate's mean in the control group from the covariate's mean in the treatment group. For example, in the pooris experiment, the researcher measured the diameter of the dough prior to cooking. In this case, the treatment group pooris had an average diameter of 4.380, while the control group had an average diameter of 4.433. The difference is therefore 0.053. This difference will be our *test statistic*, our observed indication of covariate imbalance. Perfect balance would imply a difference of zero, but by chance we expect some amount of imbalance.

The next step is to calculate the probability that the random assignment process generated a test statistic this large or larger (in absolute value). In this example, we want to figure out the probability that the assignment process generates a test statistic larger than 0.053 or smaller than –0.053. We can figure this probability out with a high degree of precision by repeating the random assignment process a large number of times, each time recording the test statistic. The `ri2` package in R makes this kind of simulation easy. Applying the package to this example, we find the following results for 100,000 simulated random assignments:

```
# Y is pretest Diameter and Z is random assignment
Y <- c(4.4, 4.5, 4.1, 4.7, 4.5, 4.2, 4.6, 4.6, 4.1, 4.5,
       4.4, 4.5, 4.7, 4.3, 4.6, 4.2, 4.3, 4.4, 4.7, 4.0,
       4.7, 4.7, 4.0, 4.6, 4.3, 4.2, 4.1, 4.5, 4.5, 4.3)

Z <- c(0, 1, 1, 1, 1, 0, 1, 0, 1, 1, 0, 0, 0, 1, 1,
       0, 1, 1, 0, 0, 0, 0, 0, 0, 0, 1, 1, 0, 1, 1)
dat <- data.frame(Y, Z)

library(ri2)
declaration <- declare_ra(N = 30, m = 15)   # 30 pooris, 15 in treatment
ri2_out <- conduct_ri(Y ~ Z, data = dat, declaration = declaration,
                  sims=100000, progress_bar = TRUE)
summary(ri2_out)
```

The probability appears to be 0.57. In other words, under the null hypothesis that the treatment and control groups truly were formed by random assignment, there is a 57 percent chance of obtaining a test statistic this large in absolute value. The conventional standard for "concern" about covariate balance is a probability of less than 0.05. We therefore do not reject the null hypothesis of random assignment; instead, we infer that the observed degree of covariate imbalance falls within the expected range.

If you obtain a probability lower than 0.05, check your procedures – maybe you made a transcription or programming error? Maybe you lost some data?

If you are evaluating covariate balance for several covariates, anomalies are more likely to occur by chance. If you are conducting multiple tests, use a threshold that is 0.05 divided by the number of covariates you are inspecting. In other words, if you are examining balance for five covariates, consider probabilities of 0.05/5 = 0.01 cause for concern.

APPENDIX 3.2: SAMPLE CLASS ASSIGNMENT

Conduct a small experiment *not* involving human subjects.

Describe the design and results in a concise 750–1,000-word essay. You are encouraged to conduct an experiment along the following lines:

1. Product Testing
2. Cooking
3. Growing plants
4. Testing physical principles (e.g., the speed with which different solutions freeze)
5. Understanding how online algorithms respond to different input

Do not do anything harmful, dangerous, cruel, or unethical. If you are uncertain about whether your experiment is questionable on any of these counts, err on the side of caution and find a different design. I would also discourage the testing of patently silly propositions (e.g., whether singing to plants helps them grow); strive to learn something meaningful from this exercise.

Your experiment should involve approximately 30 subjects. Do not spend an inordinate amount of time or money gathering data; the point of this exercise is to learn the mechanics of designing, executing, and describing an experiment.

Your write-up should contain the following:

1. A brief description of the motivation for the current study and the central hypothesis to be tested.
2. A brief description of the subjects, randomization procedure, treatments, setting, and outcome measures.
3. A brief discussion of whether the three core assumptions are likely to be satisfied.
4. A figure or table describing the distribution of individual outcomes, by experimental condition.
5. A statistical analysis of the results. Interpret as precisely as possible the estimated ATE and its estimated standard error.
6. A brief conclusion summarizing the findings and their implications.
7. An appendix with your data and accompanying R program.

Register your pre-analysis plan on Open Science Framework (OSF) online repository before you conduct your experiment. (If you do not already have an OSF account, create one for free at osf.io.) Submit an electronic version of your write-up by the due date via OSF by making your essay, the data, and the code public.

4

A Tour of Social Science Experiments

In Chapter 2, we defined experiments as research studies in which subjects are assigned at random to treatment or control conditions. Chapter 3 set the mechanics of random assignment in motion via a humble product-testing experiment. That exercise was meant to solidify your understanding of how to design and deploy an experimental intervention, create a database, and estimate the average effect of the treatment on outcomes. The next step is to apply the experimental method to the study of social phenomena.

Before trying your hand at a social experiment, first get a sense of how social scientists have used experiments to learn about cause and effect. Although these experiments all share a common ingredient, random assignment, they vary widely in their substantive focus. One aim of this chapter is to call readers' attention to the breadth of topics that lend themselves to experimental investigation.

Another aim of this chapter is to illustrate the design choices that researchers make when balancing their eagerness to learn against practical and ethical constraints. Some researchers opt for laboratory studies conducted under tightly controlled conditions; others opt for experiments conducted in naturalistic settings, perhaps with some loss of control over whether subjects take the treatment they are assigned. As we will see, what an experiment can teach us depends on its design.

Special attention must be paid to four aspects of an experimental research design: Who the subjects are, what interventions they are exposed to, the context in which the intervention takes place, and the way in which outcomes are measured (see Box 4.1). An important skill is to be able to read a research study and succinctly describe these four design elements, each of which has implications for what the experiment can teach us.

This chapter begins with a brief overview of the four main types of experiments. Next, in order to highlight the key ingredients that go into lab, survey, field, and naturally occurring experiments, we discuss an instructive example of each type of design. Boxes 4.2–4.5 provide other illustrative examples to inspire you as you work toward conducting your own experiment with human subjects (Chapter 6).

Box 4.1 Things to Look for When Summarizing an Experimental Design

What is the research hypothesis? What question does the researcher seek to answer?

What are the experimental conditions? What intervention does the treatment group receive? How does it differ from what the control group receives? If there are multiple treatment groups, in what ways do the treatments differ from one another?

Who (or what) are the subjects? How were the subjects chosen or recruited? Do the subjects have any characteristics that might make them especially responsive (or unresponsive) to the treatment? Are the subjects aware that they are being studied?

How are the subjects randomly allocated? What procedure determines who receives treatment? Is random assignment conducted and implemented by the researcher or by some other entity?

In what context does the experiment take place? Is the context artificial, or is it a setting in which participants ordinarily encounter the treatment? Are there any features of the setting that might be expected to accentuate or diminish the effect of the treatment?

How are outcomes measured? Are surveys, administrative data, or direct observation used to measure outcomes? How much time elapses between treatment and outcome measurement? Are outcomes assessed unobtrusively?

How do the researchers estimate the average treatment effect? Do they calculate a difference-in-means? Or compare change scores? Or do they use another statistical technique, such as regression (see Chapter 7), that adjusts for one or more pre-treatment covariates?

4.1 OVERVIEW OF LAB, SURVEY, FIELD, AND NATURALLY OCCURRING EXPERIMENTS

Experimental designs reflect trade-offs. What are the research objectives? What are the practical or ethical constraints?

If you care primarily about influencing human behavior in a given setting, your experimental design choices may favor options likely to produce practical insights that apply directly to the setting you care most about. If you are studying how to increase voter turnout in an upcoming election, for example, you might prefer that your experimental participants be people who are eligible to vote in the next election, and you might opt to study interventions that are likely to be deployed by actual campaigns (such as knocking on the doors of registered voters to tell them about the election). Conducting an experiment "in the field" is a way to shorten the distance between the experimental setting and the settings to which you hope to generalize.

On the other hand, if your primary aim is to speak to a broad theoretical question, such as why people participate in politics, you might be less focused on eligible voters or an upcoming election. Your aims could be met by studying forms of political participation such as environmentally conscious shopping, that anybody could engage in. You might reason that the theoretically relevant inducements to participation are most clearly conveyed in a lab setting, where people receive them without distractions. The lab is ideal for deploying theoretically nuanced interventions in a fairly uniform manner. The fact that you can verify that participants actually received the treatment adds another level of quality control that may not be possible in field settings.

Not everyone has the resources – space, staff, access to a subject pool – to conduct lab research. An alternative is to conduct experiments online. Some online experiments are akin to field studies in that they examine how interventions affect online behaviors, whether they be social media posts, donations, or gameplay.[1] Most online research, however, examines how people respond to surveys. Survey experiments vary the content of the questionnaire, the response options, or the order in which questions are asked. The advent of online "labor markets" has made it possible to recruit large numbers of survey respondents quickly and inexpensively.[2] An even less expensive option is to recruit people you know to participate – this low-budget option is frequently used by students (see Chapter 6 for an example).

A final design option is to assemble data from a randomized experiment that has been conducted by a government or other entity. This kind of experiment is sometimes called a naturally occurring experiment because it happens in the wild rather than under a researcher's direction. Common examples are government-run lotteries that determine who wins a large sum of money, a visa, a parcel of land, or subsidized health care.[3] One advantage of studying naturally occurring experiments is that they are often conducted on a vast scale – far beyond what researchers could afford. Another advantage is that an entity such as a government agency is responsible for providing or withholding treatment, which reduces some (but not all) of the ethical burdens on the researcher (see Chapter 5). When studying naturally occurring experiments, the main challenges are reconstructing the exact procedure by which the random assignments occurred and tracking outcomes among those who won or lost the lottery. In other words, for a study to qualify as a naturally occurring experiment, a researcher must know which subjects were allocated to each experimental condition and must be able to verify that the allocation was random.[4]

Having described some of the main types of experimental settings, let's now delve more deeply into each category in order to get a sense of what each type of experiment looks like in practice.

4.2 LAB EXPERIMENTS

Since the 1940s, the lab has frequently been used to study how mass media shapes what people think about social and political issues.[5] In order to appreciate the details of how

[1] See Parigi et al. (2017) for an overview of online experiments. Some noteworthy examples include Munger (2017) and Siegel and Badaan (2020), which study experimental interventions aimed at curbing inflammatory rhetoric by Twitter users, and Doleac and Stein (2013), which examines discrimination in online resale markets.

[2] See Berinsky et al. (2012), Teschner and Gimpel (2018), and Coppock and McClellan (2019) on the behavior of experimental participants recruited from online labor markets and survey aggregators.

[3] See Kuhn et al. (2011) on cash lottery prizes, Hall et al. (2019) on a land distribution lottery in the Antebellum South and its effects on slave ownership and fighting for the Confederacy, Clingingsmith et al. (2009) on visa lotteries allowing a pilgrimage to Mecca, and Finkelstein et al. (2012) on the Oregon Medicaid lottery.

[4]   Other scholars use the term "natural experiment" to include studies that do not involve random assignment. For example, studies that examine the effects of wars, treaties, famines, and natural disasters have all been called natural experiments despite the fact that none of the interventions are randomly allocated.

[5] Prominent examples include studies that examine the effects of television news on what viewers consider the most important issues facing the country (Iyengar et al. 1982), the effects of negative campaign advertisements on viewers' intention to vote (Ansolabehere and Iyengar 1995), or the effects of televised political

Box 4.2 Examples of Lab Experiments

Experiments that take place under lab conditions are often classified according to whether the lab is housed in an office building, usually on a college campus. Traditional lab studies invite participants to visit the lab in person. One variation is to invite participants to a virtual lab, from which they interact with the lab staff and other participants from some remote location via computer connection. Another variation is a so-called lab-in-the-field, whereby a research team sets up lab equipment (e.g., computer monitors) in an off-campus location, such as a shopping center.

An example of a traditional lab experiment is Hayran et al.'s (2020) study of FOMO (fear of missing out). Students in a summer school course were recruited to come to a lab, where they were randomly assigned to one of two conditions. Those in the FOMO treatment group "read about how other students were spending their summer vacation," with accompanying photos featuring destinations that are popular among students. The control group read general information about the university with accompanying photos. The central hypothesis, which the data support, is that the FOMO treatment diminishes the value that people place in their current activity (summer school) and makes them less eager to attend summer school the following year.

Although most lab experiments recruit students as participants, researchers sometimes attempt to recruit participants from the broader community. For example, McClendon and Riedl (2015) report the results of a lab study conducted in Nairobi in which local residents listened to audio clips of sermons from different Christian sects. The hypothesis is that self-affirming content typical of sermons delivered in Pentecostal churches promotes political action. Outcomes were measured by examining whether participants sent a text message to a local organization that urges residents to share their views about government performance and policy priorities. Exposure to self-affirming sermons increased the rate at which participants sent messages.

Many social science lab studies draw inspiration from economics and present participants with choices about how to allocate money. Participants' allocation choices reveal something about what they value, such as the well-being of others. A commonly used lab activity is a strategic "game" that a participant plays with another person (real or imagined). Iyengar and Westwood (2015) recruited 815 people to play two such games online, the "trust" game and the "dictator" game, to measure how they feel about other players of varying age, gender, income, race, and party affiliation.[6] (The other players did not actually exist; their profiles were randomly generated by the experimenters.) The researchers used the amount of (real) money allocated to other players to measure outgroup hostility toward members of the other party and to those of a different race. Players allocated substantially more to co-partisans than out-partisans; ethnicity, on the other hand, seemed to have little effect on allocations.

---

debates that feature "uncivil" exchanges between candidates on viewers' trust in government and politicians (Mutz and Reeves 2005). In each of these studies, experimental participants were invited to a lab setting and shown programs with randomly varying content, sometimes over the course of several visits. Participants then completed a questionnaire that measured outcomes. In the latter two examples, participants were also recontacted weeks later to complete a follow-up interview.

[6] The authors write: "In the trust game, Player 1 is given an initial endowment ($10) and instructed that she is free to give some, all, or none to Player 2 (said to be a member of a designated group). She is further informed that the researcher will triple the amount transferred to Player 2, who will have a chance to transfer an amount back to Player 1 (though Player 2 is under no obligation to return any money). The dictator game is an abbreviated version in which there is no opportunity for Player 2 to return funds to Player 1 and where the amount transferred is not tripled by the researcher. Since there is no opportunity for Player 1 to observe the strategy of Player 2, variation in the amount Player 1 allocates to different categories of Player 2 in the dictator game is attributable only to group dislike and prejudice" (p. 701).

Lab-in-the-field studies are conducted under controlled conditions but not housed in a traditional lab setting. For example, in their study of perspective-giving, Bruneau and Saxe (2012) arranged an exchange of perspectives between 47 Caucasian Americans who were native English-speakers and 76 Mexican immigrants who were native Spanish-speakers, the majority of whom were undocumented. All participants were recruited from Arizona, an American state that borders Mexico. American participants came to a lab site at the local public library, while Mexican participants came to a lab site at a local community organization. Participants were randomly assigned to be Senders or Receivers. Senders were instructed to "write on one or two of the most difficult problems or greatest barriers facing people from your ethnic group in this country." Each Receiver was instructed to translate a putative Sender's essay "using Google Translate, and write a summary of the translated essay in their own words." (p. 858). In actuality, the Sender's essay was written by a confederate writing from a standard script (p. 858). Outcomes were assessed by a post-intervention survey that measured positive and negative attitudes about the outgroup. Compared to Caucasian message senders, Caucasians who received messages expressed more positive opinions about Mexicans.

lab experiments are designed and executed, let's take a close look at "Entertainment-Education Effectively Reduces Prejudice," by Murrar and Brauer (2018).

Serialized entertainment programs attract large and attentive audiences. It is widely believed that such programs have the potential to change attitudes about social groups or issues. For example, then-Senator Joe Biden opined in 2012 that the mid-1990s TV series *Will and Grace*, which featured gay characters and presented them in a sympathetic light, "probably did more to educate the American public than almost anything anybody's ever done so far." Murrar and Brauer (2018) set out to study attitude change toward another stigmatized group, Arab Muslims. Their experimental intervention is the sitcom *Little Mosque on the Prairie*, a show set in a small Canadian town that attempted to portray Muslim Arabs in an endearing way. Let's review the key ingredients of their study.

Hypothesis: The authors' central hypothesis is that "Interacting with and getting to know members of an outgroup," such as Arab Muslims, "allows individuals to relate to that outgroup more, to extend their sense of self to that outgroup, to understand the perspectives of the outgroup members, and to identify more closely with the outgroup" (p. 1055). Although watching a sitcom falls short of "interacting" with Arab Muslims, it does allow the audience to get to know them as individuals, thereby challenging negative group stereotypes.

Treatment and Control Conditions: The experimental intervention was exposure to six episodes of *Little Mosque*; those in the control condition were instead exposed to six episodes of the popular sitcom *Friends*. The authors explain what they regard as the key theoretical ingredients of the treatment:

Little Mosque ... was written to increase understanding of Western Muslims and the issues they face as a community by focusing on a group of Arabs/Muslims residing in a small Canadian town. The characters are depicted as relatable and likable people who face common everyday experiences (e.g., disagreeing with parents, interacting with a love interest, or planning an event). They come off as normal people who have flaws and positive attributes just like everyone else in the world. In this way, the characters are easy to identify with. Additionally, they vary in age, gender, beliefs, lifestyles, and occupations, expanding the range of viewers who may find them relatable. *Little Mosque* also depicts intergroup contact between Muslims and non-Muslims (mostly White Christian characters) that audience members may relate to and mimic in their own lives. (p. 1058)

The control sitcom *Friends* also presents likable characters working through everyday situations, but it "exclusively depicts White characters going about their daily lives" (p. 1058). To quantify this contrast between the two programs, the authors "counted the number of times a White character said something to a character from a minority group, or vice versa ... *Little Mosque* had an average of 206 cross-group utterances per episode, while *Friends* had none" (p. 1059). The authors go one step further to confirm that the two sitcoms were otherwise similar. A separate group of 49 White undergraduate students were recruited to watch either *Little Mosque* or *Friends*; these viewers rated the two sitcoms' characters similarly in terms of how "funny, relatable, interesting, annoying, realistic, understandable, likeable, and agreeable" they were. In sum, the two sitcoms have many similarities, but only the treatment sitcom exposes the audience to likable Arab Muslim characters.

Recruitment of Participants: The authors sought to recruit White participants, since the *Little Mosque* was designed to dispel Whites' negative views about Arab Muslims. These participants were drawn from two sources, using different inducements: "Fifty-eight of the participants were recruited through local advertisements in grocery stores, doctor offices, and university buildings in a mid-sized Midwestern city and were paid $20 for participating ... The other 135 participants were students recruited to receive extra credit in their introductory psychology course" (p. 1058). These participants were screened to ensure that none had previously watched *Little Mosque*.

Random Assignment: Although the authors do not provide details about how they conducted the random assignment – were participants randomly assigned one-by-one as they arrived at the lab? – they do state clearly that random assignment was used: "individuals from student and nonstudent samples were randomly assigned to watch an entertainment–education television sitcom designed to reduce prejudice toward Arabs/Muslims, or a control sitcom" (p. 1057). They also verified that, as expected, the treatment and control groups had similar background attributes, such as age and gender. The researchers also measured attitudes toward Arabs/Muslims before showing the treatment or placebo episodes, and these baseline attitude profiles look similar in both experimental groups.

One potential threat to random assignment is attrition, or the failure to obtain outcome measures from all participants. Random assignment ensures that the *assigned* treatment and control groups are comparable; however, if some participants disappear before outcomes are gathered, the remaining members of the treatment and control groups may no longer be comparable. Attrition did not occur during a post-treatment survey conducted immediately after participants watched the sitcoms, but approximately 20 percent of the participants failed to complete a follow-up survey four to six weeks later (p. 1058).

Instructions to Participants: Like many psychological experiments, this lab study attempts to conceal the research hypothesis and the experimental manipulation. As the authors explain, "To reduce experimental demand effects, a White experimenter told the participants that the purpose of the study was to examine television-watching behaviors and that they would be watching one of 12 possible sitcoms" (pp. 1060–1061). The term "demand effects" refers to the notion that participants might feel pressure to express views that confirm the research hypothesis. By exaggerating the number of possible sitcoms, the experimenter led the participant to think that *Little Mosque* was just one of many sitcoms, not the focus of the study; moreover, the vague term "television-watching behaviors" drew attention away from the true purpose of investigating attitude change about Arab Muslims.

One challenge in implementing this experimental design is the sheer amount of time it takes to watch six episodes of a sitcom. The authors explain that "The study took about two and a half hours to complete. Participants were given short breaks to prevent fatigue" (p. 1061). Other experiments using a similar design have either had participants attend one fairly long screening of serialized entertainment (Green et al. 2021) or invited participants to a series of shorter screenings on multiple occasions (Paluck 2009; Banerjee et al. 2019). The latter approach is a bit closer to how people ordinarily watch sitcoms but risks losing participants who fail to show up to scheduled screenings. Although watching a medley of episodes in a lab setting is somewhat artificial, the lab allows the researcher to verify that participants did view these programs.

Measuring Outcomes: Because the central hypothesis is that *Little Mosque* changes Whites' attitudes toward Arab Muslims, outcome measurement focused primarily on assessing participants' perceptions of and feelings toward "Arabs," "Arab people," and "Arab Muslims." One measure asks participants to rate their warmth toward various groups, including Arab people, on a thermometer that ranges from 0 ("extremely cold") to 100 ("extremely warm"). Another measure assessed "how likable or unlikable you find the groups." In addition, the post-treatment survey includes a battery of questions about resentment, such as "Arabs are getting too demanding in their push for equal rights."[7] The researchers also assessed participants' "implicit" attitudes toward Arab Muslims by measuring the speed with which participants can classify pairs of words.[8] Such tests are thought to reveal the automatic positive or negative orientations that people harbor toward groups. A final outcome measure is behavioral in the sense that it asks respondents, "How much time would you be willing to volunteer for an organization that works to protect the civil rights of Arabs?" Responses on a five-point scale ranged from 1 = "less than 1 hour per week" to 5 = "7 or more hours per week."

This rich collection of outcomes makes it easier to detect the effects of the treatment. Although any single measure might provide an unreliable indication of how a participant feels about Arab Muslims, all the measures taken together give a fairly precise indication.

---

[7] Yet another series of questions probed respondents' assessments of whether Arabs are warm, aggressive, self-centered, or hard-working, as well as the extent to which different Arabs vary along these dimensions.

[8] To get a feel for how implicit attitude measurement works in practice (and to take a test yourself), google "project implicit."

The downside of presenting respondents with so many questions about Arab Muslims is that those in the treatment group can see the connection between the sitcom episodes they watched and the questions asked afterwards. The concern is that some treated participants may exaggerate their warmth toward Arab Muslims, which would in turn cause researchers to overestimate the apparent influence of viewing the *Little Mosque* episodes. This concern may be less acute when participants are reinterviewed four to six weeks later, as memories of the viewing experience fade. Although logistically challenging, this follow-up interview is a very important feature of this study, as it poses less of a threat to symmetry and allows the researchers to assess whether the effects of *Little Mosque* subside over time.

Checking for Covariate Balance: The authors measured attitudes toward Arab people during the baseline interview (before participants watched the sitcoms). Although random assignment ensures that the treatment and control groups have the same *expected* potential outcomes, the baseline interview helps researchers establish that the two groups in fact have similar profiles. Prior to viewing the sitcoms, the average feeling thermometer rating of Arab people was 64.4 in the treatment group, as opposed to 64.1 in the control group. These figures imply that the assigned treatment group was only slightly more favorably disposed toward Arabs prior to exposure to *Little Mosque*.

Results: In order to assess whether *Little Mosque* changed viewers' attitudes immediately after they watched the sitcoms, the researchers compare average outcomes in the treatment group (N = 95) to average outcomes in the control group (N = 98). These results are summarized in Table 4.1. The thermometer ratings of Arabs average 64.2 in the control group (essentially unchanged from the baseline) and 70.5 in the treatment group (a gain of 6.1 points). The fact that the authors also measured how participants rated other groups, such as Whites, helps rule out the possibility that exposure to *Little Mosque* elevated ratings toward all groups; the authors find little difference between treatment and control groups' ratings of Whites, whether before the intervention or afterwards.

The measure of implicit attitudes also suggests a treatment effect in the expected direction, although the outcome is scaled in a way that makes interpretation challenging. The Implicit Association Test (IAT) is coded so that larger numbers mean more bias against Arab Muslims The researchers find that the average IAT score in the treatment group is –0.10 while the control average is 0.07, a pattern consistent with the expectation that *Little Mosque* reduced hostility. The authors report that the standard deviation of the IAT is 0.37 in the control group, which implies that the treatment moved participants about (–0.10 – 0.07)/0.37 = 0.46 standard deviations. The treatment also seems to have diminished resentment toward Arab people (2.49 in the treatment group, as opposed to 2.67 in the control group), although this difference seems less dramatic than the change in IAT scores given that the standard deviation in the control group is 0.88. The one outcome that does not seem to move in the wake of treatment is the average amount of time that a participant is willing to volunteer. The five-point volunteering scale averages are 1.44 in the control group and 1.48 in the treatment group. The standard deviation in the control group is 0.69, so the treatment effect is scarcely noticeable given the amount of variability in outcomes.

TABLE 4.1. *Baseline, midline, and endline outcomes, by TV sitcom assignment (entries are means, with standard deviations and numbers of observations in parentheses)*

Measure of Prejudice	Control at Baseline	Treatment at Baseline	Control Immediately after Viewing *Friends*	Treatment Immediately after Viewing *Little Mosque*	Control Four to Six Weeks Later	Treatment Four to Six Weeks Later
Warmth toward Whites	76.79 (SD = 18.55) (N = 95)	75.37 (SD = 18.99) (N = 95)	77.47 (SD = 18.95) (N = 89)	75.81 (SD = 19.29) (N = 86)	77.79 (SD = 17.25) (N = 70)	75.89 (SD = 19.44) (N = 84)
Warmth toward Arabs	64.11 (SD = 20.97) (N = 95)	64.37 (SD = 20.03) (N = 95)	64.16 (SD = 21.64) (N = 89)	70.52 (SD = 18.55) (N = 86)	65.29 (SD = 19.76) (N = 70)	70.30 (SD = 17.98) (N = 84)
Implicit Association Test			0.07 (SD = 0.37) (N = 91)	-0.10 (SD = 0.47) (N = 94)	0.03 (SD = 0.45) (N = 59)	-0.11 (SD = 0.37) (N = 65)
Resentment toward Arabs			2.67 (SD = 0.88) (N = 91)	2.49 (SD = 0.78) (N = 88)		
Willingness to Volunteer			1.44 (SD = 0.69) (N = 89)	1.48 (SD = 0.73) (N = 86)		

Interestingly, the follow-up interview four to six weeks later revealed that the changes in thermometer ratings and implicit attitudes persisted more or less unabated. For example, the treatment group's thermometer rating averaged 70.3, as opposed to 65.3 in the control group.

Reflections on the Study: The Murrar and Brauer (2018) study features several attractive design elements:

1. The treatment and placebo sitcoms were broadly similar except for the active ingredient, scenes involving likeable Muslim Arab characters.
2. The lab setting allowed the researchers to verify that participants indeed watched the assigned shows.
3. Outcomes were measured extensively, allowing the researchers to pinpoint how participants were affected and for how long.
4. The baseline survey confirmed that the randomly assigned treatment and control groups, as expected, had similar background attributes and attitudes.
5. Participants were drawn from two different groups, allowing the researcher to verify that the results apply to both students and nonstudents.

At the same time, the study also has some limitations that invite us to think about ways to improve the research design:

1. The viewing conditions were artificial; perhaps participants watched the sitcoms more attentively because they knew that they were part of a research study. Can you think of a way to have participants watch sitcoms under more naturalistic conditions, without jeopardizing your ability to make sure they actually watch the assigned sitcoms?
2. The lengthy set of post-treatment questions about Arabs and Muslims may have tipped off respondents in the treatment group to the purpose of the study. Perhaps the authors could have concealed the purpose of the study by having fewer questions about Arab Muslims and interspersing them with other irrelevant questions. Can you design an experiment to test whether these alternative measurement approaches produce different conclusions?
3. About 20 percent of participants did not complete the endline survey that was conducted roughly one month later. How might you achieve higher completion rates?
4. The study uses deception insofar as participants were misled about the number of sitcoms that were being evaluated. Was deception necessary? Can you think of ways to conceal the purpose of the study without misleading subjects?

4.3 SURVEY EXPERIMENTS

The term "survey experiment" refers to a random assignment study that takes place in the context of an opinion survey. Survey experiments fall into two categories. The first is an experiment in which some aspect of the survey itself is randomly manipulated. For example, a researcher might vary the order in which questions are asked or the way in

---

Box 4.3 Examples of Survey Experiments

Here are two examples of survey experiments that use variations in question wording, question order, or response options:

1a. Since the 1970s, the General Social Survey in the US has varied the wording of its question on social welfare spending.

> We are faced with many problems in this country, none of which can be solved easily or inexpensively. I'm going to name some of these problems, and for each one I'd like you to tell me whether you think we're spending too much money on it, too little money, or about the right amount. Are we spending too much, too little, or about the right amount on [Welfare / Assistance to the poor]?

> Americans, especially Whites with conservative racial attitudes, are much more supportive of "Assistance to the poor" than "Welfare" (Smith 1987; Green and Kern 2012).

1b. More elaborate experiments vary several aspects of question wording simultaneously. For example, Hainmueller and Hopkins (2015) present online survey respondents with two potential immigrants and ask which one they "prefer to see admitted to the United States." The profiles of the immigrants are rotated randomly so that the resumes that respondents see list different countries of origin, professions, language skills, and so on. The authors find that respondents, regardless of party, share clear preferences over which kinds of immigrants are most appealing: highly educated professionals who are fluent in English.

Here are two examples of survey experiments that randomly expose some respondents to an intervention midway through the survey, in order to assess the effects of the intervention on responses to subsequent questions:

2a. Panagopoulos et al. (2020) seek to assess the extent to which Democrats' and Republicans' consumer preferences change when they learn the partisan sympathies of corporations. Survey respondents were presented with a quiz about popular food chains and retail stores; correct answers raise respondents' chances to win gift cards. When they learn, for example, that the hamburger chain Wendy's recently "gave 93% of their total political contributions to Republican candidates," Democrats become less likely to want a gift card for Wendy's than for other hamburger chains, while Republicans become more likely.

2b. Many survey experiments have respondents watch treatment or control videos before answering questions that assess the extent to which the videos change attitudes or beliefs. For example, Mullinix et al. (2021) present respondents from a national survey with actual videos of lethal or nonlethal use of force by law enforcement officers before assessing respondents' beliefs about the frequency with which police use excessive force and their support for requiring that police wear body-worn cameras. The authors find both videos augment concerns about excessive force and increase support for body-worn cameras.

---

which questions are worded. The second category encompasses experiments in which some form of intervention occurs during the course of a survey interview. For example, in the article discussed in Section 4.2, Murrar and Brauer conducted a second study in which survey respondents in the treatment group were exposed to a four-minute music video featuring a diverse array of Muslims disclosing endearing things about themselves. Notice that the latter type of survey experiment is akin to an unsupervised lab study in which participants in some remote location encounter a stimulus during the course of a survey and thereafter answer questions that serve as outcome measures. Because the latter type of design has much in common with a lab study, we will focus here on the former type in this section. The example we present next is a survey that presents respondents with differently worded questions.

Barber and Pope (2019) investigated the extent to which the public follows the cues of prominent political figures when expressing support for various government policies. The rise of Donald Trump as a presidential candidate in 2016 and incoming president in 2017 provided an unusual opportunity to study cue-taking because, as the authors document, he at various times expressed diametrically opposing positions on 10 issues, ranging from abortion to gun control. What happens when survey respondents are informed of his stated position on one side of an issue or the other?[9]

Hypothesis: Republicans who are informed of Trump's stated issue positions, be they liberal or conservative, will become more inclined to side with them.[10] This hypothesis has a number of noteworthy elements. First, it applies only to those who, when asked about their party affiliation prior to the experimental intervention, described themselves as Republicans. Second, the hypothesis predicts that Republicans will follow Trump's lead regardless of its ideological direction. In order to evaluate this claim, the authors present some respondents with liberal Trump cues, some with conservative Trump cues, and some with no cues.

Treatment and Control Conditions: Respondents were presented with questions about an assortment of political issues.[11] In the control condition, the issues were stated without reference to Trump. For example, the question on abortion reads as follows: "Do you support or oppose enforcing penalties on women who obtain abortions?" Respondents assigned to the Liberal Trump condition instead encountered the question, "Donald Trump has said that he opposes such penalties. How about you? Do you support or oppose enforcing penalties on women who obtain abortions?" Respondents assigned to the Conservative Trump condition saw the opposite cue: "Donald Trump has said that he supports such penalties. How about you? Do you support or oppose enforcing penalties on women who obtain abortions?"

Notice the importance of having a pure control group. A comparison between Liberal Trump and Conservative Trump conditions could establish that cues matter, but it would be unclear whether both cues matter or only one. For example, one could imagine a result in which Republicans who received the Liberal Trump cue were

---

[9] Because the positions reported to respondents were actually expressed by Donald Trump, the authors were able to vary the cues in a survey conducted in January 2017 without providing false information.

[10] For ease of exposition, we have simplified the authors' hypotheses, which also address whether less knowledgeable Republicans are especially susceptible to Trump-related cues.

[11] The 10 issues are raising the minimum wage, increasing taxes on the wealthy, punishing women who have abortions, immigration policy, guns on school property, the Iran nuclear deal, universal health care, background checks for gun purchases, climate change, and funding Planned Parenthood. Due to an error in the survey, the conservative cue was not presented before the question on immigration policy.

consistently more liberal in their expressed issue stances than those who received Conservative Trump cues. Does that mean that the liberal cues moved Republicans in a liberal direction or that they stayed put while conservative cues moved their counterparts in a conservative direction? A pure control group allows the researchers to figure out which Trump cues cause a change in responses.

To establish that Republicans follow Trump's cues rather than those of Republican leaders in general, the authors added another experimental condition that presents the cue of "Congressional Republicans." For the abortion question, this cue says, "Congressional Republicans have said that they oppose such penalties." Depending on the issue, this cue is sometimes in a liberal direction and sometimes in a conservative direction, reflecting the actual position of Republican congressional leaders.

Recruitment of Participants: Survey respondents were provided by YouGov, a firm that conducts online opinion research and periodically administers surveys to a nationally representative set of adults. Because YouGov surveys the same people repeatedly, the authors obtained background information about respondents (e.g., age, ethnicity, party affiliation) from prior surveys (p. 42). The advantage of conducting the survey through YouGov is that the survey organization recruits a nationally representative cross-section of American adults, which is to say that they share the same demographic profile as the American population.

Random Assignment: Of the 1,300 respondents, 500 were assigned to the control condition, 200 to the Liberal Trump condition, and 200 to the Conservative Trump condition. The remainder were assigned to the Congressional Republicans cue.

One subtle feature of this experiment is that each respondent remained in the same experimental condition across all 10 issues. For example, a respondent who received a Liberal Trump cue on the issue of abortion also received a Liberal Trump cue on the issue of raising the minimum wage.[12]

Outcome Measures: For each issue, respondents were asked to indicate whether they supported the policy, opposed the policy, or "Don't Know." Notice that the presence of the latter option forces the researcher to make a choice when coding the outcome. The authors analyze their data after excluding those who say Don't Know, but this approach might slightly distort the apparent effects of cues if respondents become less likely to choose Don't Know after receiving a cue.[13] So when analyzing their data, we will present results including all three response options.

---

[12] One might speculate that the ideological consistency of the Trump cues made them more credible. The authors do not indicate whether the policy questions were presented in random order. If they had been, one could test whether the Liberal or Conservative Trump treatment became stronger based on the number of policy questions that preceded it.

[13] For an example of how different rates of don't know responses might distort our inferences, consider the following case. In the control group, 50 percent support, 40 percent oppose, and 10 percent don't know; in the treatment group, 60 percent support and 40 percent oppose. If we exclude don't know responses, 56 percent of the control group respondents appear to support the policy, which understates the difference in support between treatment and control groups.

TABLE 4.2. *Support for enforcing penalties on women who have abortions, by experimental condition and party affiliation*

Republican Respondents Only

	Liberal Trump (Opposes)	Conservative Trump (Supports)	GOP Leaders (Oppose)	Control
Support	25.7	43.6	16.7	30.6
Oppose	52.7	29.0	67.5	45.6
Don't Know	21.6	27.4	15.9	23.9
Total	100.0	100.0	100.1	100.1
N	74	62	126	180

Non-Republican Respondents Only

	Liberal Trump (Opposes)	Conservative Trump (Supports)	GOP Leaders (Oppose)	Control
Support	12.7	10.9	11.0	10.0
Oppose	66.7	77.5	74.1	72.2
Don't Know	20.6	11.6	15.0	17.8
Total	100.0	100.0	100.1	100.0
N	126	138	274	329

Results: Table 4.2 presents results for the abortion issue by experimental condition. (Interpreting results for other issues will be left as an exercise.) The upper panel of the table focuses solely on 442 Republican respondents, as they are the ones the authors predict will respond to Trump-related cues. Among Republicans in the control condition, 30.6 percent support punishing women who have had an abortion, while 45.6 percent oppose, and 23.9 percent don't know. The Liberal Trump cue reduces support to 25.7 percent and increases opposition to 52.7 percent. The Conservative Trump cue increases support to 43.6 percent while driving opposition down to 29 percent. Interestingly, the liberal cue conveyed by Congressional Republicans also promotes opposition, in this case raising it to 67.5 percent.

Do cues from either Trump or Republican leaders affect non-Republicans? The lower panel of Table 4.2 reports the results for the 858 respondents who call themselves Democrats or Independents. Among non-Republicans, only 10 percent of the control group favors penalties for women who have abortions, and this number scarcely changes across the experimental conditions. In the Conservative Trump condition, support rises to only 10.9 percent. The liberal cues conveyed by either the Liberal Trump condition or the Congressional Republican condition, oddly enough, also produce a small increase in support for penalties. Compared to Republican respondents, non-Republicans seem much less responsive to cues from either Trump or Congressional Republicans.

Reflections on the Study: The Barber and Pope (2019) study features several attractive design elements:

1. The four experimental conditions allow the researchers to isolate the extent to which Republicans were influenced by Trump endorsements, as opposed to endorsements from other Republican leaders, and to show the extent to which

Republican participants followed Trump's cues, whether they pointed in a liberal or conservative direction.

2. The study involves a national sample of Republicans and covered a broad array of issues.

3. The researchers avoided using deception insofar as the competing cues associated with Donald Trump were inspired by his actual statements.

One limitation of the study is that it does not assess whether the cues have a lasting effect on participants' opinions.[14] Since the study was conducted as part of the YouGov panel survey, it would have been possible to reinterview the participants, albeit at additional cost. Doing so would have shed light on the question of whether cues embedded in survey questions affect responses only to that question and then disappear. If that were the case, cues would only have an enduring effect on public opinion if they were continually restated by party leaders or mass media.

4.4 FIELD EXPERIMENTS

Field experiments attempt to assess the effects of an intervention under naturalistic conditions. Where possible (and ethically permissible), researchers try to make their study unobtrusive – participants are unaware that they are in a research study and act as they ordinarily would. Interventions tend to be realistic in the sense that they are the treatments that are actually deployed in the world: Regulations, persuasive messages, incentives, instructional programs, and so forth. Outcomes are often measured using administrative data, again to minimize participants' awareness of and involvement in the data collection process. Examples from several social science disciplines may be found in Box 4.4.

This form of research has become especially common in studies of political campaign tactics, with literally hundreds of experiments assessing the impact of appeals conveyed via mass media, digital media, mail, or face-to-face communication (Green and Gerber 2019). One of the most elegant experiments was conducted by Nickerson (2008), who sought to test the effects of nonpartisan encouragements to vote. Teams of canvassers visited registered voters at their homes and urged them to vote in an upcoming municipal election. The design of the study enabled the researcher to assess not only the effectiveness of the voting appeal on the people who spoke directly with a canvasser but also the spillover effects on other voters living at the same address.

Hypothesis: Face-to-face encouragements to vote in an upcoming election increase voter turnout rates. Those who speak with canvassers directly about the upcoming election are more likely to vote, as are other eligible voters living in the same household who do not speak with canvassers directly.

---

[14] Nor does it attempt to establish what respondents thought Trump's positions were prior to receiving the cues, although the authors did find especially strong cuing effects among Republicans whose knowledge about politics was relatively limited.

Box 4.4 Examples of Field Experiments

A large and growing number of field experiments are conducted each year in economics, political science, sociology, communications, and criminology. The following thumbnail sketches give a sense of the breadth of topics that can be studied using this experimental approach.

Reducing intergroup conflict: Mousa (2020) conducted an experiment in post-ISIS Iraq designed to reduce hostility between Christians and Muslims. She created a soccer league in a largely Christian community in which some teams were assigned to have some Muslim players during the two-month season. Four months later, the study assessed whether random exposure to Muslims led Christian players to view them more positively and to have more cross-group social interactions.

Policing tactics: Sherman and Rogan (1995) conducted an experiment to study the effects of police raids on drug-dealing locations. Raids were authorized by court orders at 207 locations, of which 104 were randomly assigned to be raided by teams of uniformed police. The hypothesis is that fewer crime reports would occur on the 104 blocks where raids were assigned relative to the 103 blocks where raids were possible but not ordered. Raids seemed to have little effect on subsequent crime in the vicinity of the drug-dealing locations.

Government corruption: Peisakhin and Pinto (2010) studied the extent to which bribery plays a role in whether New Delhi's slum dwellers are able to obtain a ration card that entitles them to food subsidies. The authors recruited 86 people who were eligible for ration cards and randomly varied how they applied to receive them. Some paid a bribe, some received assistance from a nongovernmental organization, some made a Freedom of Information Act request, and some simply applied. The outcome is whether each applicant received a ration card and, if so, how quickly. Assistance did little; freedom of information requests were more effective; bribes worked best.

Experiences and attitude change: As discussed in Chapter 1, Balcells et al. (2022) randomly assign Chilean undergraduates to attend a museum that commemorates the human rights abuses of the military dictatorship that ruled the country. Outcomes – views about democratic institutions – were measured via a survey administered shortly after the trip and again six months later. Attending the museum did increase "satisfaction with democracy," although this effect faded months later when participants were reinterviewed.

Treatment and Control Conditions: In both the treatment and placebo conditions, canvassers visit the homes of registered voters and knock on the door. At an address assigned to the treatment condition, if a registered voter answers the door, the canvasser delivers a get-out-the-vote appeal and a leaflet about voting. At an address assigned to the placebo condition, if a registered voter answers the door, the canvasser delivers an encouragement to recycle household trash and a leaflet about recycling. The assumption is that this placebo message about recycling has no effect on turnout.

This placebo-controlled design focuses on people who answer their doors when canvassers knock. Door-answerers in the treatment group will be compared to door-answerers in the recycling group. Absent a placebo-controlled design, the analysis would be much more complex, because only a small portion of the doors that canvassers visit result in actual contact. In other words, only a small share of the households assigned to receive the treatment actually receive it. This problem is termed *noncompliance* with treatment assignment. The placebo-controlled design addresses the noncompliance issue and keeps the analysis simple, just the usual difference-in-means.

Recruitment of Participants: Public records indicate who is registered to vote and where they reside. The researcher compiled a list of addresses in which precisely two registered voters reside. Participants were unaware that they were part of a research study.

Random Assignment: The list of two-voter households was randomly divided into three groups. The treatment group was visited by canvassers and encouraged to vote; the placebo group was visited by canvassers and encouraged to recycle; and the control group was not visited.[15]

Checking Covariate Balance: Nickerson (2008) reports that the observable characteristics of treatment and placebo households are very similar. They have similar age profiles, and they voted at similar rates in previous elections. Importantly, their rates of responding to a knock on their door were similar as well. The last comparison is reassuring, as the design calls for a comparison between door-answerers who hear the get-out-the-vote appeal and door-answerers who hear the recycling appeal.

Instructions to Participants: Because the study did not recruit participants in any overt manner or involve them in a survey, no instructions were provided.

Outcome Measures: Public records indicate which registered voters in each household cast ballots in the municipal election. Because canvassers took note of who answered the door, their turnout can be looked up, as can the turnout of their housemates.

Results: Table 4.3 presents the comparison between the treatment and placebo groups. Among those who answered the door and received an encouragement to vote, turnout was 39.1 percent. Among those who answered the door and received an encouragement to recycle, turnout was 29.8 percent. The difference between 39.1 percent and 29.8 percent is 9.3 percentage points, implying that for every 100 people who discussed voting at the door, an additional 9.3 cast votes.

What about registered voters who did not come to the door when the canvassers visited? The rightmost columns of Table 4.3 indicate that their voting rates, too, were elevated when canvassers discussed the coming election with their housemate. Turnout was 34.7 percent among registered voters whose housemates discussed the coming election with canvassers, as opposed to 28.9 percent among registered voters whose housemate discussed recycling with canvassers. This difference amounts to 5.8 percentage points.

---

[15] Only the vote and recycling conditions are required for estimation, but the control group helps verify that the placebo-controlled design was implemented properly, as explained in footnote 16.

TABLE 4.3. *Voter turnout by treatment assignment, by whether the participant spoke directly to a canvasser or not*

	Directly Reached by Canvassers		Housemates Not Reached by Canvassers	
	GOTV Message	Recycling Message	GOTV Message	Recycling Message
% Who Voted	39.1	29.8	34.7	28.9
N	486	470	484	470

Reflections on the Study: The Nickerson (2008) study features several attractive design elements:

1. Outcomes were measured unobtrusively, using publicly available records indicating who voted.
2. The experimental design allows the researcher to estimate the effects of talking with a canvasser about the upcoming election instead of talking with a canvasser about recycling.
3. The experimental design also allows the researcher to estimate the spillover effects of having a housemate who talks with a canvasser about the upcoming election.
4. The fact that treatment and recycling groups were contacted at similar rates also helps establish that door-answerers in the treatment and placebo conditions are comparable.[16]

One limitation of this study is that the design leaves open the question of why the spillover effect occurs. Is it that door-answerers who discussed the coming election with canvassers relayed the message to their housemates? Or is it that the housemates saw the leaflet that canvassers left behind with the people who answered the door? Although the leaflet adds an element of realism, eliminating the leaflet would have more directly pointed to intra-household conversations as the source of apparent spillovers.

4.5 NATURALLY OCCURRING EXPERIMENTS

The distinction between field experiments and naturally occurring experiments is subtle. Naturally occurring experiments are conducted by governments or nongovernmental organizations, rather than by researchers. (Sometimes the two categories overlap, as when researchers help an organization orchestrate a lottery.) Because so many governments and organizations allocate resources via lottery, the range of applications is quite broad, as illustrated by Box 4.5.

---

[16] The inclusion of an untreated control group allows the researcher to verify that the placebo had no effect on voting. In this study, those assigned to the placebo group (including those who were not reached at the door) did not have elevated turnout compared to the assigned control group.

Box 4.5 Examples of Naturally Occurring Experiments

Although researchers do not design these experiments or conduct the interventions, they play a key role in reconstructing the random assignments and measuring outcomes. These examples illustrate the breadth of applications.

Pilgrimage to Mecca: Clingingsmith et al. (2009) use the lottery that allows Pakistanis to travel to Mecca to study how the pilgrimage affects the attitudes of those selected to make the journey. Outcomes among those who do or do not win the lottery are assessed via a survey that assesses their observance of Islamic practices, views about gender equality, and attitudes toward other ethnic groups. Results suggest that the pilgrimage makes them more accepting of gender equality and more supportive of harmonious relationships with non-Muslims.

Military service and criminal activity: Galiani et al. (2011) study Argentina's draft lottery, which randomly assigned men to military service based on the last three digits of their national ID. Linking administrative records, the authors compare the rates of subsequent criminal activity among drafted and undrafted men of the same age. Drafted men were more likely to subsequently acquire a criminal record than undrafted men.

Roommates and BMI: Frijters et al. (2019) studied a men's college in Kolkata, India to assess whether a students' weight is affected by the weight of their assigned roommate. Roommates are randomly assigned without regard to their body mass index (or their caste), but this information is gathered when they arrive at the college. Weight was measured by survey enumerators for almost all students two years after their arrival. The authors find that, on average, the heavier one's roommate, the lower one's own weight.

Health insurance and health outcomes: Finkelstein et al. (2012) studied an Oregon lottery that gave uninsured low-income adults an opportunity to apply for Medicaid. Outcomes such as health care utilization are measured using administrative records from hospitals and credit reports, and self-reported physical and mental health is measured using a mail survey sent to the treatment and control groups a year later. Lottery winners used more medical services, incurred less medical debt, and reported better physical and mental health than the control group.

One noteworthy example of a government-run lottery occurred in the West African country of Benin. Like many countries in this region, Benin has experienced rapid deforestation. A quarter of its forested acreage disappeared between 1990 and 2015. One proposed solution is to shore up farmers' property rights. By clarifying where parcels of land begin and end, legally enforceable land titles are thought to give farmers an incentive to farm cleared plots more intensively rather than encroaching on public forested areas. Using this approach, Benin rolled out a land registration program that demarcated landholdings, documented usage rights, and adjudicated disputes. Researchers Wren-Lewis et al. (2020) assembled data on outcomes and performed a statistical analysis.

Hypothesis: Shoring up property rights in rural areas reduces the rate of forest loss.

Treatment and Control Conditions: Starting in 2009, villages randomly assigned to the treatment group received the land registration program. The program was implemented as planned in 98 percent of the treatment villages. The control group received no program.[17]

Recruitment of Participants: Approximately 1,200 villages applied to be part of the land registration program, but only 575 met the eligibility criteria. The authors report that the eligible villages were especially rural, ethnically diverse, and prone to land disputes (p. 4).

Random Assignment: Of 575 eligible villages, 300 were selected for treatment via public lottery. A total of 80 such lotteries were held, two in each region.

Instructions to Participants: Village leaders were encouraged to apply to participate in the registration program and were aware of the public lottery. Villagers were not aware that deforestation would be monitored remotely via satellite (see Outcome Measures).

Covariate Balance: The authors verified that villages' pre-treatment attributes, such as ethnic composition, rainfall, poverty, and annual number of fires, were similar in treatment and control groups.

Outcome Measures: For the period 2009–2017, the authors assembled satellite images indicating the extent of forest coverage in the vicinity of each village and compared it to the amount of forest coverage prior to the experiment (2000–2008) in order to calculate the percentage of forest that had been lost. Rates of forest loss in the treatment group could then be compared to rates of forest loss in the control group. In addition, the researchers used satellite images to count the apparent number of fires in each location, as fires are typically used to clear forest land for farming. The prediction is that, relative to control villages, villages assigned to the land registration program experience fewer fires and a slower rate of forest loss.

One concern about land registration programs is that they could incentivize pre-emptive land clearing before registration goes into effect. The authors look for pre-emptive clearing by comparing treatment and control villages shortly after the registration plans were announced but before they were implemented.

Results: Satellite images of the 300 treatment villages and 275 control villages suggest that land registration did not encourage preemptive deforestation prior to implementation.

After implementation, the average number of fires was lower among treated villages. The annual rate of forest loss averaged 1.8 percent in the control group, as opposed to 1.5 percent in the treatment group. Although the intervention slowed the rate of forest loss, the magnitude of the effect appears to be relatively modest; the 300 treated sites together conserved a few square miles of forested land as a result of the intervention.

Reflections on the Study: The Wren-Lewis et al. (2020) study features several attractive design elements:

---

[17] Wren-Lewis et al. (2020, p. 2) report that initially the program was expected to be extended to the control group over time, but no expansion of the program actually occurred. The authors also report that 2 of the 275 control villages were treated inadvertently (p. 4).

1. The study leverages public lotteries to illuminate an important policy debate.
2. Satellite images are used to measure outcomes (forest loss and the annual number of fires) objectively and unobtrusively.
3. Outcomes are tracked over a long time period, providing a sense of the long-term benefits of the program, while ruling out the concern that land registration led to pre-emptive land clearing before the announced policy went into effect.

The main limitation of this study is the inherent ambiguity of coding forest loss and fires using satellite images. The authors note that some instances of repeated widespread fires may reflect the seasonal operation of a plantation rather than land encroachment (p. 6). Ideally, satellite-based measurements would be confirmed by teams on the ground, but deploying observers is more expensive and may expose them to personal risk given the sensitivity of land disputes.

4.6 CONCLUSION

The studies summarized in this chapter attests to the breadth of topics that have been studied using randomized experiments. Although I have drawn examples from lab, survey, field, and naturally occurring experiments, hundreds of worthy studies have gone unmentioned. Readers seeking to read more deeply may wish to consult handbooks and literature reviews in political science (Druckman and Green 2021), economics (Banerjee and Duflo 2017), sociology (Baldassarri and Abascal 2017), psychology (Shadish and Cook 2009; Parigi et al. 2017; Paluck et al. 2021), criminology (Farrington et al. 2020), education (Raudenbush and Schwartz 2020), law (Greiner and Matthews 2016), and other fields.

EXERCISES

The datasets used in the exercises are available from the book's webpage: https://osf.io/b78je/, or you may import them directly into R by installing the package `experimentr`.

4.1 Using the `murrar` dataset, answer the following questions:
    a. Create a baseline variable representing the pretreatment difference in thermometer scores for Arabs and Whites. Do the same for the first posttest. Plot these two variables, putting the posttest difference score on the vertical axis and the pretest difference score on the horizontal axis. Add some jitter to the pretest score so that you can see all the points. Do higher-than-average pretest scores tend to be associated with higher-than-average posttest scores?
    b. Plot the posttest difference score (vertical axis) and the treatment assignment (horizontal axis, adding some jitter). Does the treatment group appear to have higher difference scores, on average, than the control group?
    c. Calculate average posttest difference scores for the treatment group and the control group. Calculate each group's standard deviations. Estimate the average treatment effect and its standard error. Calculate the 95% confidence interval. Interpret the results.

d. Calculate the *change* in difference scores from baseline to posttest. In other words, subtract the baseline difference score from the posttest difference score. Again, estimate the ATE, its standard error, and the 95% confidence interval using change scores. How do the results using change scores differ from the results you obtained using raw different scores?

e. IAT scores measure reaction times – in particular, how quickly respondents recognize positive or negative stimuli after being primed to think about Arabs or Whites. The IAT score, then, represents a way of assessing negative attitudes toward Arabs *relative* to Whites. (Higher IAT scores imply more hostility toward Arabs.) Explain the conceptual distinction between the difference in thermometer ratings for Arab people and White people, on the one hand, and IAT ratings of Arab Muslims versus Whites on the other. To see whether the two scores are related empirically, plot the thermometer difference scores (horizontal axis, with jitter) and the IAT scores (vertical axis). Do higher-than-average thermometer difference scores seem to coincide with lower-than-average IAT scores?

4.2 The Bruneau and Saxe (2012) study described in Box 4.2 includes a number of noteworthy design features. Explain the purpose of each one:

a. This study does not have a pure (untreated) control group. Instead, the authors have all participants take a baseline survey, at which point they are assigned to either a perspective-giving task or a perspective-taking task. When assessing the effects of these treatments, the authors calculate the change in scores from the baseline to the endline. One concern with this approach is that scores might simply drift over time, as participants become more comfortable with answering survey questions. To address this concern, the authors measure negative attitudes toward an irrelevant group, Arabs, from baseline to endline. Using the `bruneau` dataset, assess whether attitudes toward Arabs changed appreciably between baseline and endline. What do you infer from the observed amount of change?

b. Rather than ask an identical set of questions in the baseline survey and the endline survey, the authors scattered 9 key prejudice measures amid a total of 56 questions, most of which were "filler" questions on personality or about irrelevant groups, and only 34 of the 56 questions were repeated in the endline survey. Why intersperse the questions of interest among filler questions? Why not use the same set of questions for both baseline and endline?

c. Rather than present participants assigned to the "perspective-taker" condition with the actual essays written by "perspective-givers" from the other ethnic group, the researchers used a single essay conveyed by a confederate, not an actual participant. What are the advantages of showing participants a single essay rather than an array of actual essays? Are there any disadvantages?

d. Using the `bruneau` dataset, compare the average treatment effect of perspective-giving versus perspective-taking for White participants. Calculate the 95% confidence interval for the ATE. Repeat these calculations for Mexican participants. What do you infer about the direction and magnitude of the ATE for each group?

4.3 Barber and Pope (2019) advance the hypothesis that information about Donald Trump's issue positions will have a larger effect among those who identify themselves as Republicans than among Democrats or Independents. Evaluate this hypothesis using survey responses about the issue of background checks for gun purchases. The Liberal Trump condition reads as follows: "Mandating background checks on all weapons purchases. Donald Trump has said that he supports this policy. How about you? Do you support or oppose mandating background checks on all weapons purchases?" The Conservative Trump condition said "opposes" instead of "supports." The Republican Leadership condition also said "opposes." Using the `barber` dataset, answer the following questions:

a. Focusing solely on Republican respondents, produce a table showing how rates of support for background checks differs by experimental condition. Your table should report the number of respondents in each experimental condition and the percentage of respondents who support the policy, as in Table 4.2. Interpret the results.

b. Produce the same table, this time focusing solely on non-Republican respondents, as in Table 4.2. Are the effects of the Trump treatments, as predicted, larger among Republicans than among non-Republicans?

c. Which cues are more influential for Republican respondents: Trump's conservative stance on background checks or Republican congressional leaders' conservative stance?

4.4 The survey experiment conducted by Mullinix et al. (2021) presents online respondents with text-only, video-only, or text-plus-video depictions of controversial uses of police force. Respondents saw one of two (actual) police encounters with Black motorists, one resulting in the driver's death and the other in severe injury. Outcomes included measures of respondents' emotion (feeling angry, anxious, upset), attitudes toward police, and beliefs about excessive force. Use the dataset `mullinix` to answer the following questions.

a. Those participants who were assigned to view a video were warned that it contained graphic content: "The video shows a controversial altercation between a police officer and a civilian, and this may be uncomfortable for some people to watch. If you do not feel that you can watch the video in its entirety, just continue forward in the survey." Judging from the time they spent on the video before advancing to the next screen, many viewers did seem to skip much of the content. Suppose that the researchers had not allowed respondents to skip the video; do you think that the estimated effects of the video treatments would have been stronger or weaker?

b. Focusing solely on the control group and the three treatment groups involving the lethal use of force, calculate average responses for each experimental group to the question, "To what extent do you approve or disapprove of the way the police in the United States are doing their job?" (1 = strongly disapprove, 7 = strongly approve). Estimate the effect of text-only versus control. Estimate the effect of video-only versus control. Estimate the effect of text-plus-video versus control. Are the effects "additive" in the sense that the effect of text-only plus the effect of video-only equals the effect of text-plus-video?

4.5 Balcells et al. (2022) randomly assigned 502 Chilean students to attend a museum commemorating the abuses of Pinochet's dictatorship. The authors point out that not all of the students who were assigned to attend the museum or a control activity actually showed up: "Both treatment and control consisted of 251 assigned individuals. 143 individuals assigned to treatment (57%) and 126 individuals assigned to control (50.6%) showed up at their assigned time. Both subjects who turned up and those who did not were unaware of their treatment assignment."

a. If students failed to show up on the day of the excursion but were unaware of their treatment assignment, does the random assignment assumption still hold for the students who did show up? One way to check whether the random assignment assumption was jeopardized by attrition is to examine whether the 143 students in the treatment group have similar background profiles to the 126 students in the control group. Use the `balcells` dataset to compare the following attributes, which were measured during the pre-test: age, gender, ideology, economic situation, political interest, religiosity, museum visits, trust in government, satisfaction in government, whether they think inequality is a problem, positive emotions, and negative emotions. Create a table that shows the means and standard deviations for both the treatment and control groups. Do the two groups seem to have similar background attributes?

b. In order to assess whether this experience had enduring effects, the authors attempted to reinterview students 1 week later, 8 weeks later, and 24 weeks later. As time went on, students stopped answering the surveys. The final survey gathered responses from 131 of the original 269 students. Using the same list of background attributes as above, again examine whether those in the treatment group who responded to the final survey had similar background attributes as those in the control group who responded to the final survey.

4.6 Sherman and Rogan (1995) tested whether shows of force by police deter nearby crime. Of the 207 illegal drug distribution sites that police were authorized to raid, 104 were assigned to treatment (raid) and the rest to control (no raid). One outcome measure was the number of "calls for service" from local inhabitants that police received on the city block where the raid (or potential raid) occurred. The hypothesis is that if raids deter crime, the number of calls that police receive will decline in the wake of a raid.

a. If police raids cause local residents to become more hesitant to report crime, the core assumption of symmetry may be jeopardized. Would this asymmetry in reporting lead the researchers to overestimate or underestimate the average treatment effect?

b. The variable `CFS_after_5weeks` indicates the average weekly crime rate on each block during the five weeks *after* the block was eligible for a raid. Compute the average weekly number of crimes on treatment blocks and control blocks. Use these averages to estimate the average treatment effect of raids on weekly crimes per block. Estimate the standard error and the 95% confidence interval. Do raids seem to reduce calls for service?

c. Sometimes those who evaluate police tactics do not have the luxury of analyzing a randomized experiment. Instead, they attempt to draw inferences about the effectiveness of a tactic such as raids by tracking whether crime rates seemed to subside after raids occur. *Focusing solely on blocks in the treatment group*, Table 4.4 shows the average crime rates, week by week, for 10 consecutive weeks. Weeks 2–5 were prior to raids, which occurred during week 6. Weeks 7–10 suggest whether crimes increased or subsided after the raids. Based on this table, would you conclude that crime increased or diminished, on average, after the raid?

d. Table 4.5 shows the same statistics, this time for the control blocks, where no raid occurred. Based on this table, would you conclude that crime increased or diminished, on average, after the *non*-raid? What do these tables suggest about the reliability of over-time comparisons?

4.7 Wren-Lewis et al. (2020) evaluate the effects of randomly assigned land demarcation on deforestation in Benin. As explained in Section 4.5, their study used satellite images to assess forest loss from 2001 to 2017. The intervention started in 2009. In order to keep the analysis simple, we focus attention on the 51 regions in which a lottery assigned half of the locations to treatment and half to control. The `wrenlewis` dataset contains data from these 51 regions.

a. One way to analyze this experiment is to focus on the period from 2010 to 2017. Compare the average number of hectares of forest loss in treated areas

TABLE 4.4. *Weekly crime rates for treated blocks*

	Obs	Mean	Std_dev
Week 1	104	2.923077	3.800083
Week 2	104	2.759615	3.179104
Week 3	104	3.250000	3.955456
Week 4	104	2.855769	3.230372
Week 5	104	3.346154	4.221464
Week 6 (raid)	104	3.538462	4.487140
Week 7	104	2.798077	3.734852
Week 8	104	2.865385	3.894377
Week 9	104	3.086538	4.138642
Week 10	104	3.201923	4.797612

TABLE 4.5. *Weekly crime rates for control blocks*

	Obs	Mean	Std_dev
Week 1	103	2.679612	3.916315
Week 2	103	2.737864	4.172649
Week 3	103	2.679612	3.506894
Week 4	103	3.058252	3.316108
Week 5	103	2.941748	3.920347
Week 6 (no raid)	103	3.116505	4.323445
Week 7	103	2.621359	3.275328
Week 8	103	2.475728	3.336796
Week 9	103	2.970874	4.081177
Week 10	103	2.970874	4.018234

to the average number of hectares of forest loss in untreated areas. Calculate the ATE, its standard error, and a 95% confidence interval.

b. Another way to analyze this experiment is to create a change score: Subtract the number of hectares of forest loss from 2001 to 2009 from the number of hectares of forest loss from 2010 to 2017. Calculate the ATE, its standard error, and a 95% confidence interval. Referring to the formula for estimating the standard error, explain why change scores give more precise estimates of the ATE than the raw scores used in part (a).

5

Research Ethics and Experiments Involving Human Subjects

Before you attempt your own experiment involving human participants, familiarize yourself with the laws, regulations, and norms that pertain to this kind of research. This chapter provides an introduction to the special considerations that come into play when a researcher studies how people think or act. If you are affiliated with a university or government agency, you may be expected to fulfill additional requirements, such as completing training modules and declaring any conflicts of interest.[1] Consider this chapter a starting point for further consultation with your mentors, supervisors, or colleagues.

This chapter begins by reviewing some of the experiments that led to calls for regulatory supervision. We then discuss the ethical concerns that are embodied in the so-called Common Rule, which regulates human subjects research in the United States. Even where this regulatory system does not apply, researchers are nevertheless expected to minimize risk of harm to participants, make no use of coercion, and safeguard confidential information. Next, we consider other legal and regulatory constraints on research activities. We conclude by discussing scientific research ethics more broadly, focusing on issues of transparency and disclosure.

5.1 EXPERIMENTS THAT LED TO CALLS FOR REGULATION OF HUMAN SUBJECTS RESEARCH

Regulation of social science research traces its origins to the aftermath of World War II, when revelations about the grotesque experiments conducted by Nazi doctors led to calls for ethical standards in biomedical research. These experiments involved interventions such as putting prisoners in freezing sea water to measure how long it took for them to die. Experiments conducted by Nazi doctors typified two ethical breaches: Forcing humans to participate in research and deliberately exposing them to harm.

---

[1] For example, my university requires training certification from this online resource: https://about .citiprogram.org/en/series/human-subjects-research-hsr/ . It also requires me to disclose any financial interests that could be affected by my research.

A series of subsequent experiments heightened and broadened these ethical concerns. The US Public Health Service Syphilis Study at Tuskegee (Baker et al. 2005), conducted from 1932 to 1972, tracked hundreds of Black men with syphilis over the course of the disease. The men were told that they would receive free medical care in return for participation, but they were never informed of their diagnosis, and their symptoms were treated with methods known to be ineffective. The failure to treat participants with appropriate medical care inflicted harm; although the men were not coerced into participation, they were deceived about the purpose of the study and the kind of medical care they were receiving.

Harm, coercion, and deception became prominent ethical concerns among social scientists in the wake of two high-profile experiments. Milgram's (1963) experiments on obedience were designed to investigate the conditions under which participants, following an experimenter's instructions, inflicted what they believed to be severe or even lethal electric shocks to another person. The person receiving the shocks was actually an actor pretending to be harmed, but the process of acceding to or resisting the experimenter's insistent instructions was stressful for the participants. The fact that the experimenter's instructions to participants included the phrase "The experiment requires you to continue" is thought to cross the line into coercion.[2]

In contrast to Milgram's meticulously scripted experiment on obedience, Zimbardo's (1973) experiment on the behavior of guards and prisoners in a simulated prison let events unfold without a clear experimental protocol. In this study, Stanford students were assigned to be guards or prisoners in a makeshift prison in the basement of a campus building. Zimbardo himself seems to have played a role in guiding events (Le Texier 2019), which led to escalating conflict, coercion, and psychological distress until he halted the study after a few days. Both Milgram and Zimbardo informed their participants about the true purpose of the study afterwards, but the level of coercion and stress to which participants were exposed led to calls for the adoption of professional standards by academic associations, such as the American Psychological Association (Committee on Ethical Standards in Psychological Research 1973).

A few years later, *The Belmont Report* (National Commission for the Protection of Human Subjects of Biomedical and Behavioral Research 1978) laid the intellectual foundation for a formal regulatory system. Focusing on biomedical research, the Report argued that three core ethical principles must be respected.

1. Beneficence: Researchers should not harm participants and should actively seek to identify and mitigate risk of harm.
2. Respect for persons: People have the right to decide whether to participate in a research study. To make an informed decision, adults must be provided with information about risks and benefits. Participants also have the right to withdraw from a study. Special provisions must be made for those unable to give full and free consent.

---

[2] See Burger (2009) for an attempt to replicate the Milgram experiment in a manner that addresses ethical critiques of the original study. See Blass (2004, chapters 5–7) for a detailed description of the experiment and the ethical concerns it raised for Milgram and his contemporaries.

3. Justice: The burdens and benefits of research must be fairly distributed among all segments of society. When involved in a study, participants must be treated fairly and equally.

As we will see in Section 5.2, these principles loom large in the federal regulations that were put in place in 1991, which cover both biomedical and social research.

An ethical concern not directly addressed by the *Belmont Report* has to do with maintaining participants' anonymity and safeguarding any confidential information that they disclose. During the 1980s and 1990s, scholars came to realize that even when researchers did not intend to disclose names or confidential information, datasets with rich background information made it possible to discern the identities of individual participants. Growing concern about identity theft and the security of private health information coincided with increased regulatory attention to this issue.

5.2 ETHICAL CONCERNS EMBODIED IN THE "COMMON RULE"

Colleges and universities in the United States typically operate under a regulatory system guided by a section of the Code of Federal Regulations known as the Common Rule. (An annotated version of the Common Rule, highlighting key terms and provisions, is available in the online appendix.) The regulatory system it creates consists of three components. The first defines human subjects research. The second describes the institutional review board (IRB) that every research institution must convene to evaluate proposed studies before data collection. The third describes the standards that are to be used when this review board evaluates proposals for approval.

What Counts as Human Subjects Research? The Common Rule defines research as "a systematic investigation, including research development, testing, and evaluation, designed to develop or contribute to generalizable knowledge" (CFR 2018, §46.102(l)). An experiment clearly qualifies as a systematic investigation. Presumably, one goes to the trouble of crafting an experiment because one seeks to acquire some form of generalizable knowledge. The term "human subject" refers to "a living individual about whom an investigator (whether professional or student) is conducting research" and about whom a researcher obtains "information or biospecimens through intervention or interaction with the individual, and uses, studies, or analyzes the information ..." (§46.102(e1)). This definition, for example, includes experiments that use surveys as outcome measures because surveys involve an "interaction" with respondents.[3] On the other hand, the definition excludes data collection on aggregate units, such as the voter turnout rate in a county. If there is any ambiguity about whether a project qualifies as human subjects research, the institutional review board will make a determination.

Criteria Used to Evaluate a Research Proposal: Suppose that your project qualifies as human subjects research. You must submit your proposal for review before launching your study. The standards used to review your proposal hinge on two questions. The

---

[3] Interestingly, the Common Rule excludes the following from the definition of research: "Scholarly and journalistic activities (e.g., oral history, journalism, biography, literary criticism, legal research, and historical scholarship), including the collection and use of information, that focus directly on the specific individuals about whom the information is collected" (§46.102(l1)).

first is whether your study presents "more than minimal risk to subjects."[4] Studies that are thought to present more than minimal risk are reviewed with special care, usually by the full review committee rather than by administrators. Studies that present more than minimal risk require *informed consent* by the participants. They must be told about the risks in plain language, and they must be assured that "participation is voluntary, refusal to participate will involve no penalty or loss of benefits to which the subject is otherwise entitled, and [he or she] may discontinue participation at any time without penalty or loss of benefits to which the subject is otherwise entitled" (§46.116(b8)). The reviewers of your proposal will want to know how you intend to obtain informed consent – what will participants be told, and how will they indicate their consent? The second question is whether the participants "are likely to be vulnerable to coercion or undue influence, such as children, prisoners, individuals with impaired decision-making capacity, or economically or educationally disadvantaged persons" (§46.107(a)). A study with *vulnerable* participants automatically receives a stringent review. Needless to say, those new to experiments should not use experimental procedures that may be harmful, nor should they be studying vulnerable populations.

The regulations provide more leeway for studies that pose minimal risk of harm. Researchers are expected to obtain informed consent from participants, but they may apply to have this requirement lifted on the grounds that "The research could not practicably be carried out without the waiver or alteration." For example, a researcher studying the effects of online advertisements on consumer behavior might apply for a waiver on the grounds that the advertiser does not know the identities of those to whom ads are served, and thus there is no practicable way to obtain consent. If you plan to request this waiver, you (and/or your advisor) should plan to have a discussion with an IRB administrator beforehand so that you get a sense of how they judge what is practicable.[5]

Some social science studies qualify for a relatively light review. So-called benign interventions are considered exempt from review so long as they do not involve deception and do not reveal the identities of specific participants. These exempt activities include brief, harmless interventions that do not have lasting effects, such as educational tests or survey interviews, and do not involve vulnerable participants. Studies involving benign interventions must still be submitted to the IRB, which determines whether the proposal qualifies for an exemption.

---

[4] The term minimal risk "means that the probability and magnitude of harm or discomfort anticipated in the research are not greater in and of themselves than those ordinarily encountered in daily life or during the performance of routine physical or psychological examinations or tests" (§46.303(d)).

[5] As you prepare for your discussion, it might be helpful to review the relevant provisions of the *Belmont Report* (p. 7): "In all cases of research involving incomplete disclosure, such research is justified only if it is clear that (1) incomplete disclosure is truly necessary to accomplish the goals of the research, (2) there are no undisclosed risks to subjects that are more than minimal, and (3) there is an adequate plan for debriefing subjects, when appropriate, and for dissemination of research results to them. Information about risks should never be withheld for the purpose of eliciting the cooperation of subjects, and truthful answers should always be given to direct questions about the research. Care should be taken to distinguish cases in which disclosure would destroy or invalidate the research from cases in which disclosure would simply inconvenience the investigator."

Protecting Anonymity and Confidentiality: Two features of the regulatory system that have grown more stringent over time are safeguards for protecting participants' anonymity and confidential information. Reports and datasets must not enable anyone outside the research team to identify specific participants. The most basic requirement is to exclude names and identification numbers, but a further implication is that researchers should not post such extensive profiles of participants that readers could identify them based on their unique combination of attributes. The responses that participants give to survey enumerators are presumed to be confidential and must not be reported in ways that could be traced back to specific individuals. Typically, the institutional review board will ask researchers how they will de-identify and encrypt data so that anonymity and confidentiality will not be compromised.

Deception: Although the Common Rule says relatively little about the use of deception, review boards typically expect that a researcher who uses deception – perhaps misleading participants about the true purpose of the study, providing phony information as part of the intervention, or exposing participants to actors whose behavior has been scripted by the researcher – will reveal the truth to participants at the end of the study.[6] In certain cases, when the deception is unlikely to have a material or lasting effect on participants, review boards have waived this requirement.[7] If you use deception, you ordinarily would *debrief* participants about the true purpose of the study at the end of your interaction with them, dispelling misimpressions created by the use of confederates or misleading information. Be aware, however, that a substantial number of social scientists (especially in economics) categorically reject the use of deception and that some journals refuse to publish experiments that mislead participants.[8]

In sum, the Common Rule requires that researchers carefully assess and minimize risks to participants. The underlying principle of minimizing risks to participants also requires researchers to preserve participants' anonymity and safeguard confidential information. The principle of respecting autonomy is reflected in the blanket prohibition against coercing people into participation. Another manifestation of this principle is the requirement – which may be waived for minimal risk studies not involving vulnerable populations – that people will be given an opportunity to make an informed decision about whether to participate in the study. Proposals that involve deception are held to a higher standard of review, and researchers are expected to correct the misperceptions they induce.

---

[6] See Rousu et al. (2015) for a taxonomy of different forms of deception used in research.

[7] For example, this waiver has been applied to audit experiments testing for employment discrimination (Pager 2007, p. 126).

[8] See Dickson (2011) for a discussion of the different experimental norms that prevail in economics and psychology. As Ortmann (2019) notes, "Concerns about ... deception among experimental economists are typically motivated by reputational rather than ethical concerns," insofar as researchers worry that word will spread about the use of deception, undercutting their ability to convince future participants about financial payoffs and other features of their experimental designs. Psychologists routinely use deception in their experimental designs, most of which involve student subjects. Christensen (1988, p. 664) argues that "subjects who have participated in deception experiments versus nondeception experiments enjoyed the experience more, received more educational benefit from it, and did not mind being deceived ..."

5.3 NORMS BEYOND THOSE EXPRESSED IN THE COMMON RULE

The Common Rule focuses on harm to participants, but harm to non-participants should also be considered. Experiments sometimes put research staff at risk when studies are conducted in violent locations. Experiments may also have negative consequences for bystanders. For example, providing large cash supplements to randomly selected poor families in isolated rural areas may raise the price of food and other basic supplies for others living nearby.[9] Experiments could also have a corrosive effect on the functioning of institutions. For example, when email correspondence from fictitious constituents is sent to public officials to test whether they are more likely to respond to constituents of one ethnic group, public officials might become suspicious of the authenticity of all constituent emails they receive subsequently and less likely to respond to real requests.[10]

Given the Common Rule's blind spots, commentators have warned against calling the institutional review board's assessment an "ethics review" (Michelson 2016). A broader ethical review would consider a proposed study's benefits and harms to society – a difficult and perhaps contentious undertaking when there is no consensus on how to balance benefits and harms in the abstract or in regard to a specific research project that has yet to be conducted. Experiments, especially field experiments, are the subject of vigorous ethical debate, with many proposals for regulations that go beyond the purview of the Common Rule.[11] To distill several such proposals to their bare essentials, they recommend:

1. Not conducting interventions at such a large scale that societal outcomes are affected;
2. Avoiding harms to non-participants; and
3. Obtaining consent from individuals or permission/approval from groups or their representatives.

Some authors who are concerned about possibly harmful interventions (or withholding possibly beneficial interventions from the control group) draw a distinction between researchers who design and implement their own interventions and researchers who merely evaluate the effects of an intervention designed and implemented by a group, organization, or government (see Humphreys 2015). As we noted in Chapter 4 when discussing naturally occurring experiments, researchers bear less of an ethical burden when analyzing an existing intervention, although norms about research transparency (discussed in Section 5.5) still apply.

---

[9] Actual studies of this kind find price increases to be small and, on balance, find that economic benefits diffuse to others (Egger et al. 2019).

[10] Out of concern that a flood of correspondence studies might have corrosive effects, I have deliberately not chosen such studies as examples in this book, despite the fact that they are relatively easy and inexpensive for students to conduct. This concern does not apply to correspondence studies that deliberately minimize deception (see, for example, Butler, Karpowitz, and Pope (2012)) by using actual constituents writing to their representatives, but such studies are much more challenging to orchestrate.

[11] See Desposato (2015), Humphreys (2015), Whitfield (2019), and McDermott and Hatemi (2020).

5.4 OTHER LEGAL AND REGULATORY CONSTRAINTS ON HUMAN SUBJECTS RESEARCH

In addition to the question of whether a research study is ethical, there is the question of whether that study is legal. Those conducting research in countries that restrict political speech or open discussion of homosexuality, for example, must be careful about putting their research staff or their study's participants in harm's way by using survey questions or experimental interventions that touch on sensitive topics. The same goes for financing studies with funds from outside the host country; in some countries, outside funding is prohibited or tightly regulated.

In the context of the United States, the most pertinent legal constraints have to do with the tax code, which allows universities and other nonprofit organizations to receive tax-exempt donations. To qualify for and maintain this tax status, a nonprofit organization must not engage in "electioneering" – active endorsement of candidates for elective office. For example, a researcher must not use university resources to test the effects of advocacy messages on behalf of a particular candidate or political party (see Michelson 2016 for an example). Doing so potentially jeopardizes the protected tax status of a university, which would have catastrophic financial implications.

Although it may seem obvious that researchers should obey the law, studies of corruption sometimes engage in illegal behavior in order to understand phenomena such as bribery and extortion. We earlier mentioned the Peisakhin and Pinto (2010) study, which examined the extent to which routine bribery of local administrators hastened slum dwellers' access to food ration cards. Other studies of corruption include the experimental assessment of bribes demanded by traffic police in Mexico City (Fried et al. 2010) or under-the-table payments used to obtain drivers licenses in India (Bertrand et al. 2007). Researchers who engage in or promote unlawful behavior defend their studies on the grounds that they shed light on illegal activities that happen routinely. Their critics view their behavior as reckless and inherently risky for participants and others (Morton and Williams 2010, chapter 12). Again, those who are new to social science experiments should be aware of this line of research but should not embark on studies that involve illegal conduct.

5.5 TRANSPARENCY AND DISCLOSURE

When describing scientific results, what are scholars expected to disclose about themselves and their research? The most basic and widely shared norm is that researchers must disclose conflicts of interest. Are they or their family members financially connected to the group that is conducting the study? Do they have any financial ties to the intervention that is being tested? For example, a researcher might be an investor in a start-up company that sells eye-tracking devices that record what young children are looking at when they are learning to read. If this researcher were to propose an experiment to see whether eye-tracking more accurately diagnoses dyslexia than another assessment tool, a conflict of interest disclosure must accompany the proposal. And if the study were conducted, this conflict of interest must be declared in the research report.

Even where no conflicts of interest exist, researchers are expected to adhere to certain standards of transparency when describing their study and its findings. These standards are becoming formal requirements of professional associations, journals, and research organizations. Here are three examples of emerging norms:

1. The researcher must describe the intervention, setting, and outcome measures in sufficient detail that another researcher could undertake a similar study to verify the results.
2. The researcher must indicate the method used to allocate subjects to experimental groups and the numbers of subjects assigned to each group. If any subjects are lost to follow-up, these numbers must be disclosed for each experimental group.
3. Upon publication of the study, the researcher must make the (anonymized) data and code used to generate the statistical results available to others.

These guidelines are designed to help readers evaluate a study's scientific contribution and to facilitate accumulation of knowledge through follow-up research that replicates or extends the original study.

A final concern has to do with the problem of selective reporting of results. The term "publication bias" refers to instances in which certain types of experimental findings go unpublished. The most common form of publication bias occurs when an experimental hypothesis receives no support – in the eyes of journal reviewers or editors, this "null" result might be considered too banal to warrant publication. Sensing editors' bias in favor of splashy results, researchers may decide to put their effort elsewhere and leave this project in the file drawer. (This phenomenon is often called "the file drawer problem." For convincing evidence about its pervasiveness, see Franco et al. 2014). Or they might decide to fish around in the data until they find a statistical procedure that seems to generate a splashy result (Simonsohn et al. 2014). Either way, the published research literature becomes distorted, usually because studies that find their way into print overstate the magnitude of effects.[12] Across the social sciences, emerging norms urge researchers to register their experiments in searchable public archives so that scholars reviewing the literature will be able to locate unpublished studies that might otherwise go unnoticed.

5.6 ACADEMIC INTEGRITY

Whenever people create their own data, there is always some risk of fraud. Researchers, be they students or faculty or neither, may make up the outcomes so that they tell a particular story, or they may deliberately mischaracterize when and how an experiment took place. Such behavior violates fundamental norms of scientific conduct and may constitute grounds for expulsion or termination.

---

[12] One telltale sign of publication bias is that experiments with small numbers of participants tend to produce larger effects than studies with larger numbers of participants. Smaller studies must produce bigger effects in order to be seen as statistically convincing by reviewers. For examples of this pattern, see Paluck et al.'s (2021) review of hundreds of experiments testing prejudice-reducing interventions.

Widely publicized cases of fraud have led to calls for greater research transparency, such as sharing data publicly, both to detect fraud and to deter it from happening in the first place. Public-facing, date-stamped archives of research activity, made possible by online sites such as GitHub or Open Science Framework, take research transparency a step further.

In my classes, I try to discourage fraud in three ways. I remind students about the university's honor code. I require them to include the teaching assistant and me as collaborators in their Open Science Framework projects, so that we can monitor all phases of data collection and documentation. I also emphasize that I will be grading their experimental projects based on the care with which they are designed and analyzed, not on whether the results turn out to be "interesting."

5.7 CONCLUSION

Scientific research ethics is a vast and complex topic. This chapter calls attention to important concerns related to harm, coercion, deception, data protection, and transparency. Familiarity with these concerns serves as a useful starting point. Reflect on them as you read social science experiments and the ethical debates that sometimes surround them. Keep these issues in mind as you design and implement your own experiments.

A closing thought: Some ethically fraught design choices are rooted in testable empirical claims. For example, is it necessary to deceive participants about the purpose of a research study in order to obtain unbiased results? An experiment could be devised to test whether and under what conditions participants' knowledge of the study's purpose materially affects the study's results. Randomly assign some participants to know the true purpose of the study before exposing them to a treatment or placebo; assign others to the same experiment but one whose purpose is shrouded by a cover story. Does disclosing the true purpose change the results in any material way?[13] Research on the effects of controversial experimental procedures may help narrow the range of ethical debate by shedding light on contested empirical assumptions.

EXERCISES

5.1 Looking back at the study of poori cooking in Chapter 3, explain why this study does or does not qualify as an experiment involving human subjects.

5.2 Would the *Little Mosque on the Prairie* experiment (Murrar and Brauer 2018) discussed in Chapter 4 qualify for review as a "benign intervention"?

5.3 What criteria are used to judge whether a study presents more than a minimal risk of harm to subjects?

5.4 It is ordinarily considered ethically unacceptable to expose people to dangerous and addictive interventions, such as advertisements that glamorize smoking.

---

[13] The de Quidt et al. (2018) and Mummolo and Peterson (2019) experiments find that participants in economics-style lab studies and online surveys, respectively, are scarcely affected by disclosures about the purpose of the studies in which they participated.

Suppose researchers seek to study the effects of such interventions by working with advertisers who are currently using this tactic. In their response to the criticism that promoting smoking is unethical, the researchers argue that their role would be to assign half of the people who would be targeted by the ads to a control group that receives no ads. Evaluate the researchers' argument.

5.5 How is protecting confidentiality different from protecting anonymity?

5.6 Are children considered a "vulnerable" population? Explain your reasoning.

5.7 Under what conditions does the Common Rule permit experiments to go forward without participants' informed consent?

5.8 What does it mean to "debrief" a participant?

5.9 Looking back at the examples presented in Chapter 4, describe an instance in which a study used deception. In your view, was this use of deception necessary, or could the study's aims have been achieved without deception?

5.10 What kinds of conflicts of interest might arise in the context of a social science experiment?

5.11 What is the "file drawer problem"? What are its consequences?

5.12 Many famous "correspondence" studies have involved sending similar resumes in response to job postings. Hundreds of firms receive a resume, but each resume comes from a fictional person whose name suggests a particular gender and ethnicity. The outcome is whether applicants receive a reply inviting them to an interview.

a. What ethical concerns does this design present?

b. In what ways do the ethical concerns change when the correspondence study involves a fictional constituent asking a public official for help or advice?

6

Conducting Your Own Experiment Involving Human Subjects

The preceding chapters have prepared you to design your own study involving human subjects. The early chapters introduced key concepts, guided you through a product-testing experiment, presented a panorama of social science experiments, and discussed a number of important ethical concerns. Now it is time to try your hand at formulating a testable hypothesis, devising a workable design, implementing the experiment, and interpreting the results.

6.1 SOME GROUND RULES

In order to sidestep the ethical concerns raised in Chapter 5, your first social experiment should meet the standards of what the Common Rule calls "benign interventions":

1. The procedures (the intervention and outcome measurement) should present no more than minimal risk of harm to subjects. Going beyond the benign intervention standard, I would recommend that you do nothing that would present more than minimal risks to non-subjects, including yourself. For example, do not wear politically provocative slogans if doing so poses a safety concern.
2. Do not engage in any communication that conveys falsehoods. For example, do not send employers a resume from a fictional person or ask survey respondents to read a doctored news clip.
3. Your study should not involve vulnerable populations. Your subjects must not include children or others who may be unable to make informed decisions about whether to participate.
4. Obtain informed consent if you are eliciting private information. If you are conducting a survey, the information you gather should be considered confidential. Before you conduct an interview, explain the broad purpose of the study, and assure respondents that they are free to skip questions or stop altogether.
5. Any data you gather must be stored securely and, if made public, stripped of information that could identify participants.

One advantage of following these ground rules is that you will be able to ask the institutional review board at your college for an expedited review. The IRB may still have questions or concerns but, with guidance from your advisor, you should be able to address them successfully. (If you are in a country that has no institutional review process, these ground rules still make good sense.)

To this list of ethical constraints, I would add a few practical constraints. The first is that the study should be inexpensive. You will not need a substantial research budget in order to conduct a worthwhile experiment, for a few reasons. First, as explained in Section 6.2, many types of experiments cost little or nothing to implement. Second, this experiment should be considered an exploratory study; you do not need to collect enough data to settle the research question you pose. Instead, think of your project as an opportunity to learn how best to administer your intervention, recruit participants, and measure outcomes. Third, your experiment should unfold quickly after it receives IRB approval. The idea is to conduct your study over a few days or weeks so that you can write up the results before the course ends.

6.2 GETTING STARTED

Your first task is to think of a suitable research question that fits the ethical and practical constraints laid out in Section 6.1. My experience has been that students have very different tastes, not only in terms of what they prefer to study but also how they prefer to gather data. Some enjoy doing projects that involve personal interaction, while others would prefer to study people from afar. To help you brainstorm about potential projects, Table 6.1 lists several categories of projects that vary in substance and design.

The first category includes studies that promote participation in activities or events. For example, you might look to see who is on your school's slate of upcoming speakers. Perhaps you could select a target group of students and randomly urge some of them to attend in order to assess the effectiveness of your invitation on attendance. The same goes for charitable activities, such as volunteering at food kitchens, donating blood, or showing up for community service at a local park. Again, the design involves creating a list of potential volunteers and reaching out to a random subset of them in some way. Assuming that the outcome measure is attendance, you will need to think about how to identify the people who show up. Taking attendance for in-person events is easiest when your subject pool consists of people you know.[1] Taking attendance for online events is even easier but may require some coordination with the host.

A similar design involves encouraging actions such as recycling waste products, donating used eyeglasses, or conserving electricity. For example, suppose that every floor in college dorms has a recycling bin. Randomly assign half of the floors to receive some kind of encouragement to recycle, and coordinate with the janitorial staff so that you can measure the volume of recycling in each bin over the course of a week. This kind of experiment can also be conducted in residential neighborhoods; to measure outcomes, weigh the volume of recycling that residents put out for collection. See Box 6.1 for examples.

---

[1] One complication of inviting some people and not others is that they may talk among themselves. If the treatment group informs the control group of the upcoming event, you may fail to see a treatment effect, not because your invitation is ineffective but rather because the core assumption of noninterference was violated. Try, therefore, to pick a group of participants who are unlikely to transmit the treatment to one another.

TABLE 6.1. *Examples of studies suitable for course assignments*

Possible Topics of Study	Easy to Measure Outcomes?	Inexpensive?	How Long to Complete?	Prone to Implementation Problems?
Promoting Collective Action	Usually	Usually	If you are working with an existing group or campaign, 3–4 weeks	Depends on whether you must coordinate with an existing organization
Charitable or Civic Contributions	Yes	Yes	If you are working with an existing group or campaign, 3–4 weeks	Depends on whether you must coordinate with an existing organization
Tipping	Yes	Yes	Depending on restaurant or taxi volume, can be a few days	Not if you have personal ties to the waitstaff or drivers
Retail Sales	Yes	Pick an intervention that is inexpensive	If days are the unit of assignment, 1 month; faster if you can randomize across retail locations	May take a dry run or two to get the treatment, assignment, and outcome measurement to run smoothly
Surveying Student Preferences	Requires implementation of a survey	Yes, unless you plan to pay respondents	Roughly 1 week if you have cooperative respondents	Requires pilot testing, especially if the survey is conducted online
Online Behaviors (like promoting worthy kickstarters)	Usually	Yes	Depends on the intervention and outcome	Sometimes
Taste Testing or User Experience	Usually involves a ratings survey	Depends on what is to be tasted	Perhaps a single day, if participants are easy to recruit	Requires close attention to detail
Brief Pedagogical Interventions	Yes	Yes	A few days to measure retention	Requires recruitment of people seeking to acquire a given skill
Non-deceptive Variations in Everyday Activities	Yes	Usually	May take days or weeks, depending on the activity	Difficult to "blind" yourself if the activities involve personal interaction

---

Box 6.1 Examples of Experiments That Promote Environment-Friendly Behaviors

A useful summary of the experimental literature on pro-environmental behaviors may be found in Osbaldiston and Schott (2012). Their overview of more than 200 experiments categorizes the treatments according to whether they provide information, incentives, or feedback. The authors attempt to summarize which interventions have tended to produce the strongest behavioral effects. Their extensive bibliography is especially valuable if you are looking for studies to replicate or extend.

Although environment-related experiments are often conducted in field settings, some designs also include survey or lab elements. For example, Lacroix and Gifford's (2020) study of participants recruited from an online platform sought to discourage meat consumption using messages that called attention to its negative environmental consequences; this survey experiment measured outcomes by asking participants to keep a food diary over the next few weeks. Another study conducted in Singapore invited students to taste-test a new yogurt drink, but the main outcome of interest was whether participants rinsed and recycled the yogurt container, as urged by instructions posted on the wall (Rosenthal and Linder 2021).

Retail sales and gratuities are outcomes that are well suited to experimental evaluation. Many studies have tested whether sales increase when stores play certain kinds of music or diffuse certain kinds of aromas. (Section 6.3 discusses one such study.) Researchers have tested assorted tactics that waitstaff use in order to impel restaurant customers to leave larger gratuities. Experiments indicate, for example, that tips increase on average when waitstaff introduce themselves by name, compliment customers, write thank you messages on the check, or leave candies at the table (Lynn 2018).

The preceding examples involve outcomes that may be measured without burdening participants. You instead need to coordinate with store managers to track sales, online seminar hosts to track attendance, or custodial staff to track recycling volume. It helps to do a dry run of data collection before your experiment launches, just to check that the measurement process is running smoothly. Beyond that, you need not approach participants, although some researchers prefer to interview a few participants in order to conduct a *manipulation check* to verify that the treatment is being received in the way you intended. For example, if your experimental intervention involves drawing smiley faces on the back of restaurant bills, you might conduct a short survey to confirm that subjects noticed and appreciated them.

On the other end of the spectrum are experiments that require data collection from participants. Many experiments rely on survey interviews to measure outcomes. As discussed in Chapter 4, some experiments embed randomly assigned interventions in the survey itself. For example, during the course of a survey, you might present respondents in the treatment group with information about an issue or policy. The information could be conveyed by having respondents read a newspaper article or watch an instructional video. Another broad class of survey experiments investigates how responses change when questions are worded differently or when respondents are presented with different response options.

In my courses, a large proportion of students opt for survey experiments. As a skill-building exercise, survey experiments have some advantages. Students learn to develop a questionnaire; if the survey is conducted online, they may also learn to do a bit of programming in order to implement the survey (and random assignment). Further lessons will be learned as students attempt to recruit participants and obtain their informed consent.

The downside of conducting a survey experiment online is that the process tends to run fairly smoothly and invisibly, which means that students do not have to think about how to handle the contingencies that inevitably arise in the course of conducting phone or in-person surveys. And unlike lab or field experiments, students conducting online surveys tend not to glean insights from watching participants in each experimental condition as they receive and react to the treatment. If you are going down the survey route, be sure to choose a topic and experimental design that will repay your effort. Box 6.2 describes a well-crafted survey experiment conducted by students, and the online appendix provides the questionnaire, the consent form, the application to the institutional review board, and the pre-analysis plan.

Taste-testing is another form of experiment that involves face-to-face interaction. Although taste-testing requires close attention to design details, it has the advantage of being fun, which makes it fairly easy to attract an ample number of participants. Over the years, students in my classes have tested the relative merits of different coffee makers, fresh versus fresh-frozen bagels, conventional butter versus vegan butter, pasta boiled with salt versus not, and every conceivable method for cooking rice.

When designing a taste-testing experiment, one must be careful to address possible threats to the symmetry assumption. Feel free to inform participants that they are participating in a taste-testing study, but do not disclose the hypothesis or their assigned treatment condition. Beyond blinding, other design nuances require special attention. Although it may be convenient to serve the treatment dish first and gather ratings from the treatment group before serving the control dish, the problem is that the longer partici-pants wait, the hungrier they get. If the control group is hungrier than the treatment group, the ratings given to the two dishes will reflect a muddled combination of treatment effects and hunger effects. Ideally, one would conduct treatment and control tastings concurrently or in random alternation, so that hunger or the heat of the food is unrelated to the treatment one receives. Another design challenge is to prevent interference between subjects, which could occur if participants chat while tasting.

Just as taste-testing experiments attract participants looking for food and fun, educational experiments may be appealing to students seeking to learn new languages, retain scientific terminology, or expand their vocabulary. The idea is to find people who are motivated to acquire some new skill and experimentally vary their pedagogical approach. If the skill consists of something manageable, such as learning 100 vocabulary words that might appear on an admissions test for graduate school, the experiment might vary whether learners are instructed to use "rehearsal and repetition" (Banikowski and Mehring 1999) as opposed to "loci" methods whereby learners imagine a vivid narrative that places each word in a specific location (Moe and De Beni 2005). The research question is whether one learning method works better than another, both immediately after the instructional exercise and a few days later. Variations on this theme include inviting participants to watch a documentary, lecture, or drama in order to assess their effects on knowledge about a given topic.

Box 6.2 An Example of a Survey Experiment Conducted by Students

For her college term paper assignment, Grace Campbell conducted a survey experiment to assess the extent to which respondents discriminate against Republican college applicants.[2]

Campbell recruited 53 of her friends to complete a short online survey. After answering a few questions about their personal attributes, such as age, gender, and party affiliation, respondents were presented with brief profiles of two applicants. The experimental manipulation was to append to one of the two applicants' profiles an extracurricular activity that signaled an applicant's party affiliation. For example, an applicant's Democratic affiliation was signaled by listing "Volunteered for Democratic Party of Alameda County." Respondents, who were predominantly Democrats, indicated which of the two applicants they would prefer to admit to the college. Respondents repeated this exercise, evaluating two further pairs of applicants. Neither of the applicants in the second pair disclosed any partisan activity. The final pair of applicants featured one who disclosed pro-Republican activity: "Canvassed for Kevin McCarthy's (R) Congressional Campaign." Campbell found a sharp decline in support for admission when this applicant disclosed Republican ties. An applicant who would otherwise be admitted by 46 percent of respondents was admitted by only 22 percent when their profile lists volunteer work for the Republican candidate. By contrast, an applicant's disclosure of ties to the Democratic Party seemed to have no apparent effect on respondents' admission decisions.

Two years later, a team of four undergraduates replicated Campbell's experiment with some small adjustments (Zhou et al. 2021). Their online survey was completed by 66 of their friends, about half of whom identified as Democrats. A randomly selected group of respondents made choices between hypothetical college applicants, such as in Table 6.2.
The other respondents saw the same applicants but with the third extracurricular activity switched, so that now Applicant B canvassed for a Republican senator.

Zhou et al. find that a candidate who was preferred by 44 percent of respondents in the control group was preferred by only 24 percent of those who saw a resume that included canvassing on behalf of a Republican candidate. These results are similar to Campbell's.

Supporting materials, including the authors' application to the Institutional Review Board, pre-analysis plan (including R code), Qualtrics code for the online survey, data, and report may be found in the online appendix.

TABLE 6.2. *Online survey example from Zhou et al. (2021)*

Qualifications	Applicant A	Applicant B
GPA	3.8	3.95
SAT Scores	1,520/1,600	1,490/1,600
Extracurricular Activities	1. Boys and Girls Club Volunteer	1. Varsity Tennis Team Captain
	2. National Honor Society Member	2. Mock Trial Team Member
	3. Canvassed for (R) Senator Deb Fischer (Nebraska)	3. Founder of School's "High School Students for Civic Engagement Club"

If you had to select one, which of these two students would you prefer to see accepted into your University?

One final type of experiment deserves mention: A non-deceptive study that varies how you undertake ordinary tasks. For example, if you are looking to buy a car, you might reasonably wear casual clothes or business clothes; doing so in random order as you visit multiple car dealerships would allow you to test whether you are treated differently by salespeople. Similarly, if you are hunting for a job or internship, your résumé might reasonably accentuate your academic credentials or your extracurricular activities; if you were to randomly call attention to one or the other, would that affect whether you are invited to an interview? There are many reasonable ways to undertake everyday activities – tidying up the shared spaces of your dorm, posting comments online, composing thank-you notes. So long as you are pursuing a legitimate goal and not using deception, varying the way in which you conduct yourself may offer fruitful experimental opportunities.

6.3 SOME INSTRUCTIVE EXAMPLES

This section presents a thumbnail sketch of some feasible projects. These experiments are inexpensive and raise no serious ethical concerns, but they do require careful planning. The aim is to give you a sense of how small-scale experiments are designed and implemented. As you read the study descriptions, note the choices that researchers made about how to randomize the experimental intervention, measure outcomes, and maintain the credibility of core assumptions.

Aromas and Purchasing Behavior in a Café: For decades, scholars who study consumer behavior have investigated whether retail sales increase when stores or restaurants use "atmospheric" interventions, such as background music, lighting, or aromas. Some of these experiments have attracted attention in the popular press by showing, for example, that bookstore sales increased by 5 percent on days in which ambient chocolate scent was diffused in stores. Because atmospheric adjustments are typically inexpensive, any appreciable increase in sales would be a net boon to retailers.

How would one go about randomizing atmospherics? One possibility is to work with a chain store and randomly assign several of its outlets to treatment. That requires a lot of advance planning, because the researcher must coordinate with each outlet. An easier alternative is to work with a single store and randomize the days on which chocolate scent is diffused. This approach was used in the experiment conducted by McGrath et al. (2016), which took place in a Canadian bookstore-café. Each day over the course of one month, the researchers flipped a coin to determine whether scents were to be diffused during store hours.

To give the store a chocolate aroma, the researchers used a diffusing machine and heated a pan of chocolate on a stove. To verify that chocolate scent permeated the store in ways that were detectable by customers, the researchers conducted a small manipulation check. Fifteen customers were asked to respond to a brief survey, which asked whether they detected any scent and, if so, what kind. The authors report that "Six respondents spontaneously identified that ambient scent as chocolate, and another five reported recognizing the scent as chocolate once the enumerator identified the scent as such" (p. 672).

Daily retail sales constitute the study's main outcome. Sales during the 16 treated days averaged 612.00 Canadian dollars, whereas sales during the 14 control days averaged 575.39 dollars. This implies a sales increase of 36.61 dollars, or 36.61/575.39 = 6.4 percent, which is even larger than the percentage increase in sales reported in a previous study of chocolate aroma and bookstore sales in Belgium. However, the estimate of 36.61 is subject to considerable uncertainty. Its standard error is estimated to be 51.56. Although our best guess is that chocolate aromas brought in an additional $36.61 in sales each day, the 95% confidence interval ranges from –69.00 to 142.24. This study, in other words, provides a valuable experimental design and a suggestive estimate, but it does not provide conclusive evidence about whether aromas increase sales.

Tipping in Restaurants: Experimenters have tested a variety of tactics that waitstaff might use in order to impel customers to leave larger gratuities. As noted in Section 6.2, the results suggest that tips increase on average when waitstaff introduce themselves by name, compliment customers, write thank you messages on the check, or leave candies at the table.

In order to conduct a study of this kind, you either need to work as a server or know servers who would be willing to help you conduct an experiment. Cooperative servers are crucial in this type of study, as servers conduct the random assignments, deploy the treatment, and keep track of the tips that they received.

Suppose that the treatment is whether the server writes a thank you note with a smiley face on the back of the bill that is presented after the meal (Rind and Bordia 1996). The control group receives the bill in the same manner but without the thank you note and smiley face. Assuming that just one bill is presented to each table of diners, the unit of random assignment is the table. How should the random assignment be conducted? Two considerations should be borne in mind. First, if the servers are going to conduct the random assignment on the fly, they should do so in a way that does not alert customers. Waitstaff might be given pennies with different mint marks; servers would select one penny from a pocket and put a bill into the treatment group if the mint date ends in 1 and into control if the mint date ends in 0. (This method can be expanded to include as many different pennies as there are experimental groups.) A second consideration is the trustworthiness of the servers. Consciously or unconsciously, they may be tempted to give the friendly treatment to customers who might give especially large tips. If you sense that trustworthiness is an issue, you could modify the design. Randomly assign servers to write notes on all the bills they present during randomly selected *shifts*, rather than randomly selected tables. This type of assignment will give less precise estimates of the treatment effect because all the tables on a server's shift are assigned as a cluster to treatment or control.[3] Another option is for you to personally conduct and supervise the random assignment of each table. So long as you retain the physical bills for your records, you can verify that servers complied with your instructions.

Assuming data collection goes smoothly, the next question is how to define the experimental outcome. One option is to use the tip amount; another is to use the tip percentage (i.e., tip divided by the total amount paid by the customer). If the bills tend to

---

[3] See the online *R Companion* for statistical packages that take clustered assignment into account when calculating standard errors and confidence intervals.

be similar across tables, the two approaches will render similar statistical results. But if bill size varies markedly across tables, you might reflect on what quantity you most care about. Presumably, waitstaff care most about the absolute amounts that they receive; they would be disappointed if an average increase in tipping percentage were driven by generous tips on small bills but not on large bills. You might therefore decide to use the absolute tip amount as the outcome and use the bill amount as a covariate. We illustrate that statistical analysis in the exercises in Chapter 7.

Blood Donation on Campus: Our final example is broadly illustrative of experiments designed to promote positive behaviors or to discourage negative behaviors. The former includes efforts to recruit volunteers to work in soup kitchens or to read to disadvantaged children in after-school programs. The latter includes efforts to prevent jaywalking or littering.

A large experimental literature has grown up around the challenge of encouraging blood donations, especially among young adults. As Sénémeaud et al. (2017) point out, young adults constitute the ideal donor population insofar as they tend to be in excellent health, but their rates of donation tend to be lower than the adult population as a whole. The creative challenge is to come up with messages or messengers that increase blood donation rates.

The challenge from the standpoint of experimental design is to deploy the randomized intervention in a manner that provides ample data while not creating unwanted spillovers. Sénémeaud et al. (2017), for example, distributed two different kinds of leaflets in college classrooms. To be more specific, they distributed two versions of these leaflets to each class that they visited. Because they happened to know each student in the class, they could keep track of which student received which treatment. However, this design raises the concern that close friends in the same class will influence each other's decision to donate blood. Suppose that a student who receives Treatment A decides to donate blood after reading the leaflet; her friend, who receives Treatment B, would otherwise not donate blood but will now do so at her urging. The spillover effects generated by Treatment A, in other words, make both treatments appear equally effective. For this reason, it might be better to change the design so as to reduce the risk of interference. One option might be to accost students as they walk alone through campus, encouraging them to donate blood via Treatment A or Treatment B.

Another challenge is measuring outcomes. In principle, donating blood is a behavior that can be directly observed and recorded, but one must somehow create a dataset that links each person's treatment assignment to his or her blood donation outcome. Sénémeaud et al. seem to have encountered difficulties in this regard. They note that "In order to identify participants who gave blood, an experimenter attended the blood drive in order to ask each donor (after she or he had given blood) if she or he had received a flyer two weeks before the drive and, if so, which one" (p. 169). This process of asking blood donors whether they received a flyer adds an extra layer of uncertainty – do people accurately recall which flyer they received? One concern is that, although the authors report that "equal numbers of the two flyers were distributed in each class" (p. 169), they also report that 237 subjects received the control leaflet, while 217 received the treatment leaflet. It is not clear whether the manner in which outcomes were measured contributed to the imbalance between treatment and control. A better approach would be to match each blood donor by name to the master list of students who received each leaflet. That, in turn, requires learning students' names when talking to them about donating blood.

In sum, published experiments conducted in real-world settings can be instructive not only because they shed light on a particular research question but also because they convey practical lessons about how to collect all of the required information under real-world conditions.

6.4 WRITING A PROPOSAL AND A PRE-ANALYSIS PLAN

Once you have decided what to study and how, two remaining administrative tasks remain. The first is to draft a study description for the institutional review board. This process was described in Chapter 5, and the online appendix for this chapter contains an example of a student research protocol that was reviewed and approved by an institutional review board.

A pre-analysis plan is a public document that lays out what you plan to do with the data once you conduct the experiment. For the small experiments described in this chapter, this document can be fairly brief. The main elements to include are:

1. *The hypothesis (or hypotheses) you seek to test.* What do you expect to find? For example: "Diffusing chocolate aroma increases café sales." This declaration tells the reader about the purpose of the experiment.

2. *How the randomization was or will be conducted.* For example: "Each morning before the store opens, a coin is flipped to determine whether chocolate aroma will be diffused that day." This section allows the reader to confirm that the data are analyzed in a manner that follows logically from the experimental design.

3. *How outcomes will be measured.* Try to be specific. If you intend to combine more than one outcome into an index, for example, include R code that describes the procedure for creating this index.

4. *The statistical procedures that will be used to estimate the ATE, its standard error, and its confidence interval.* Again, R code is helpful here.

5. *Any specialized research questions.* Will you be looking for especially large or small effects for certain outcomes rather than others? If so, explain. For example: "Chocolate aroma is predicted to have a larger effect on café sales than on book sales." Will you be looking for especially large or small effects among certain kinds of subjects? For example: "When tipping, male restaurant customers are more responsive than female customers to smiley faces they receive from female waitstaff."

Examples of this kind of document may be found in the online appendix to this chapter.[4] The online appendix also includes instructions for posting your plan to a public registry so that others can verify that the document was date-stamped before your experiment was conducted.

---

[4] Several online sources provide guidance as to how and why to craft a pre-analysis plan. See https://egap.org/resource/10-things-to-know-about-pre-analysis-plans/ (last accessed February 26, 2022).

Of what value is a pre-analysis plan? A plan written in advance of launching an experiment can help you work through important questions, such as what is being tested and how the design addresses the hypothesis. Sometimes key details do not come into focus until one writes out the planning document. R code that is written while your experimental design is fresh in mind also helps streamline the process of analyzing the data once they become available. In addition to front-loading some of the work that goes into experimental design and analysis, a plan serves a broader scientific goal: It makes the results more credible to readers. To be precise, a pre-registered plan helps increase the credibility of results when it is *followed* by researchers. Researchers must make a deliberate choice to limit their own discretion when deciding which observations to include, how to measure outcomes, or which statistical tests to conduct.

Registering a plan is optional, and *following* the plan you have registered is also optional. But in order to reap the credibility benefits that a pre-specified plan confers, you must both compose a plan and stick by it. For that reason, when you write up the results of your experiment, you should indicate clearly whether you are following, or deviating from, the plan that you posted. Sometimes deviations are unavoidable, as when experiments run into unexpected implementation problems. Presenting unplanned analysis is okay, but you should inform readers about how the planned and unplanned results compare.

6.5 WRITING UP YOUR RESULTS

For the most part, your write-up should follow the structure laid out in Chapter 3 for describing experiments without human subjects. To that checklist, add three further enhancements:

First, an experiment involving human subjects is a more substantial undertaking, and so your introduction should be more substantial as well. Explain how your experiment builds on experiments that have come before. Are you replicating an experiment that was conducted previously? If so, compare and contrast your experimental design. Are you conducting an experimental test of a proposition that had previously been assessed using non-experimental evidence? If so, explain the advantages and disadvantages of your experimental approach. Your concluding section should return to this theme, explaining how your results inform the prior literature on your research question.

Second, discuss any ethical concerns that informed the research design or that arose in the course of conducting the study. Beyond including a specific discussion of ethics, attend to ethical concerns as you write. For example, take care not to disclose participants' identities. Do not quote them or refer to them by name without their permission. Do not describe participants in sufficient detail so that a malicious reader could figure out who they are. Protecting anonymity rules out photographs of participants or detailed maps of where they reside.

Third, the concluding section of your essay should not only summarize the substantive implications of your results but also call attention to lingering research questions and suggest possible experimental strategies for addressing them. Research on human subjects almost inevitably confronts problems of implementation – for example, participants fail to show up, do not comply with their assigned treatment, or leave the study without providing outcomes – and the concluding discussion is an opportunity for you to offer creative suggestions for improving the experimental design so as to make it more workable and informative. How might future research change the treatments, participants, contexts, or outcome measures to illuminate the conditions under which interventions are especially effective?

6.6 CONCLUSION

Conducting an experiment involving human subjects is a serious undertaking, which is why procedural safeguards must be in place to protect the wellbeing and privacy of those involved. This chapter presumes that your first social experiment will stay well away from the ethical guardrails. Fortunately, these constraints do not prevent you from studying interesting and important topics.

Creativity is required to design an experiment that is both feasible and informative. Just as aspiring artists may learn by attempting to reproduce works by accomplished artists, aspiring experimenters may learn by retracing the steps of previous experimental researchers. If you are in search of a creative spark, draw inspiration from the menagerie of experiments that can easily be found in your college's digital library or in public repositories of reprints and working papers.

A final word of advice: If possible, conduct a small "pilot test" before launching your study. Gather a small number of observations and see how it goes. If necessary, make adjustments to your design and your planning documents.[5] A dress rehearsal can make things go much more smoothly when the experiment officially gets underway.

EXERCISES

The datasets used in the exercises are available from the book's webpage: https://osf.io/b78je/, or you may import them directly into R by installing the package `experimentr`.

6.1 Suppose a classmate came to you for your opinion about the ethics of the following study. The proposed intervention involves creating a fresh user account, visiting a video-hosting site such as YouTube, and randomly varying whether a newly posted music video receives positive or negative comments. The outcome is the share of positive or negative comments from other viewers that are posted during 24 hours following the initial comment. What ethical concerns does this study raise, and what adjustments to the design do you recommend?

6.2 Robitaille et al. (2021) report the results of a study conducted at an official center that residents of Ontario must visit "in person for almost any public service including driver's license, health card, and photo identification transactions." This center attracts roughly 200 residents each day. The researchers sought to enroll visitors to the center as organ donors, and their study attempts

---

[5] A pilot study must still be approved by the institutional review board. If your experimental design changes in the wake of the pilot test, you may need to inform the IRB of your modifications before proceeding to the main data collection effort. Data from the pilot test are typically excluded from the final dataset.

to assess which kinds of appeals work best. Their design began with three days of control group appeals, followed by three days of appeals that included a promotional brochure, followed by three days altruism appeals, followed by three days of self-interest appeals, and finally three days of empathy appeals. Outcomes for each three-day messaging period were measured using administrative records showing which residents completed organ donation paperwork. Can you see any drawbacks to this design? If so, which core assumption or assumptions may be violated?

6.3 A busy gym at a large hotel wants to find a way to get more gym patrons to wipe down exercise equipment after they use it. The hotel plans to put dispensers with sanitized towels next to every machine; in addition, half the machines will be randomly assigned to have signage that reminds users to wipe down the equipment after each use. They ask for your guidance about how best to measure outcomes. Rather than station an observer in the gym to measure the use of sanitary towels, the hotel is considering measuring outcomes by counting the number of unused towels that remain beside each machine at the end of the day. Would you recommend stationing an observer or counting unused towels? What are the advantages and disadvantages of each method of measuring outcomes? Another option is to use video footage from the gym's security cameras to figure out whether gym patrons wiped down the machines they used. Weigh the advantages and disadvantages of this approach.

6.4 In Rind and Bordia's (1996) restaurant tipping experiment, waitstaff wrote thank you notes and smiley faces on bills that were randomly assigned to treatment. The researchers instructed waitstaff to deliver the bill (whether in treatment or control) without conversing further with diners at each table. Which of the core assumptions would be jeopardized by further conversation with diners after they received the bill?

6.5 Ellison et al. (2019) study efforts by campus dining halls to reduce food waste. Two similar dining halls at a Midwestern university were selected for comparison. The authors describe the research design as follows:

Student plate waste data was collected three days per week (Monday, Wednesday, and Thursday) in both the treatment and comparison dining halls during the lunch period (11:00 am–2:00 pm) for a total of thirteen weeks … [Intervention] materials were posted in the treatment dining hall beginning October 20 (Thursday of week eight) and remained in place for the duration of the study (five weeks). No educational materials were posted in the comparison site, but data collection continued in this location … (p.277)

The researchers point out that food waste at each location was discreetly weighed each day, so that diners were unaware that their behavior was being studied. The researchers further point out that the dining halls were more than a mile apart, limiting the potential for spillovers. That said, can you see any drawbacks to this design? If so, which core assumption or assumptions are jeopardized?

6.6 In their study of charitable contributions, Rondeau and List (2008) conclude that "We find evidence that challenge gifts positively influence contributions in the field, but matching gifts do not." In their field study, "A total of 3,000 Sierra Club supporters were randomly divided into four treatments. Supporters received a solicitation letter from the director of the Club, written, as usual, on Sierra Club letterhead and accompanied by a payment return card ..." (p. 256). Each letter urged recipients to donate to a fundraising effort to fund its school-based education programs. The four solicitation letters each made a different appeal. One appeal sought to raise a target of $5,000. A second appeal sought to raise a target of $2,500. A third (challenge gift) appeal explained that "$5,000 has to be raised, but ... a leading donor has already committed $2,500 in a challenge gift to the cause." A final (matching gift) letter explained that "$5,000 has to be raised, but ... a leading donor has committed to match the first $2,500 in contributions at a rate of 1:1" (p. 257). When assessing the effectiveness of these appeals, the researchers exclude non-contributors and calculate the average donation made by contributors in each experimental condition.

    a. Critically evaluate the decision to exclude noncontributors. Why might this practice lead to biased inferences about the effectiveness of different fundraising messages?

    b. Using the `rondeau` replication dataset, calculate the average donation amount for each of the four experimental conditions (without excluding noncontributors). Do these results affirm the researchers' conclusions about the relative merits of challenge and matching gifts?

    c. Without excluding noncontributors, calculate the 95% confidence interval of the effect of using a challenge appeal versus a matching gift appeal. Does this confidence interval demonstrate the superiority of challenge appeals?

6.7 Using the `mcgrath` replication dataset from McGrath et al.'s (2016) chocolate aroma study, use R to calculate the following quantities:

    a. Total sales, on average, for the 16 treatment days.

    b. The standard deviation of total sales for the 16 treatment days.

    c. Total sales, on average, for the 14 control days.

    d. The standard deviation of total sales for the 14 control days.

    e. Use the above quantities to estimate the average treatment effect, its standard error, and the 95% confidence interval.

6.8 In order to assess whether chocolate aromas increase demand for certain types of goods, McGrath et al. disaggregate total sales into three subcategories: (1) food sales in the café, (2) book sales, and (3) sales of bulk coffee, tea, or spices.

    a. Using their replication data, estimate the average treatment, standard error, and confidence interval for each of these three outcomes.

    b. Which type of sales outcome seems to be most affected by chocolate aroma?

    c. What do you infer from the fact that all three of the confidence intervals include zero?

6.9 A checklist of elements to include in a write-up can be useful to authors conducting experiments. It can also be a useful guide for summarizing a research article.

Read the McGrath et al. (2016) article (a reprint of which may be found in the online appendix), and briefly answer the following questions:

a. What is the main hypothesis?

b. What is the experimental setting?

c. What is the treatment condition? What is the control condition?

d. What are the subjects, and how are they randomly assigned to treatment or control conditions?

e. Is there a manipulation check? If so, what does it indicate?

f. What are the outcomes?

g. What are the main findings? How much statistical uncertainty remains?

h. Are any of the three core assumptions jeopardized by the design or implementation of the study?

i. How do the findings contribute to the literature in this area?

j. What ethical concerns does this experiment raise?

7

Doing More with Data

Previous chapters have stressed the conceptual underpinnings of experimental design and the practical challenges of implementing experiments that safeguard core assumptions. With these fundamentals in place, we turn our attention to more specialized topics having to do with data analysis, presentation, and interpretation.

One objective of this chapter is to introduce a statistical method, regression analysis, that can extract more information from experimental results. A second objective is to encourage the use of graphs when analyzing and presenting experimental results. This topic complements the discussion of regression, as some of the most informative graphs are those that convey how outcomes, treatments, and covariates are related. A final objective is to discuss different ways of evaluating whether an estimated average treatment effect is substantively and statistically meaningful. This topic offers a fitting note on which to close the book, because it reminds us that we may learn from experimental results even when they tell us that a treatment is ineffective.

7.1 REGRESSION

Regression is a statistical method that is widely used to analyze experimental data. An attractive feature of regression analysis is that it may improve the precision with which the average treatment effect is estimated. Just how much additional precision will depend on the empirical application, but the gains can be considerable.

This section offers a brief introduction to regression. I begin by writing down a regression equation and explaining what the terms represent. Next, I describe the algorithm that regression uses to estimate the average treatment effect. In the simplest case (i.e., when the only variables in the model are the outcome and the treatment) regression produces exactly the same estimates as the familiar difference-in-means estimator. The two estimators may diverge when regression takes account of covariates that predict outcomes. Revisiting the Murrar and Brauer (2018) experiment from Chapter 4, I use graphs to illustrate how covariates may change both the estimated ATE and the estimated standard error.

Writing Down a Regression Equation: Consider the case of an experiment with two randomly assigned conditions, treatment or control, and a numeric outcome, such as

---

Box 7.1 Notation Used in Regression Equations

Here is a dataset containing six rows. The two columns report the outcome and the assigned treatment for each participant:

Outcome (Y_i)	Treatment (T_i)
2	0
4	0
3	0
5	1
8	1
8	1

The subscript i refers to a particular row in the dataset. The expression $Y_5 = 8$ means that the fifth participant's outcome is 8. To refer to a participant's outcome without specifying which participant, we simply write Y_i. Similarly, we write T_i to refer to the treatment assigned to the ith participant.

A regression equation expresses the outcome for the ith participant (Y_i) as a function of that participant's assigned treatment (T_i) and unobserved characteristics (U_i),

$$Y_i = a + bT_i + U_i.$$

The intercept (a) and slope (b) in this equation are the unknown parameters that regression estimates by minimizing the sum of squared residuals. Of particular interest is b, the average treatment effect.

---

participants' survey ratings. The starting point for regression analysis is writing down an equation that expresses the experimental outcome variable (Y) as a function of the treatment (T) and all remaining unobserved variables (U). Each variable is subscripted with the letter i to refer to an arbitrary experimental participant. (See Box 7.1, which explains and illustrates this notation.) The regression expresses outcomes for the ith participant as follows:

$$Y_i = a + bT_i + U_i \tag{7.1}$$

In Eq. (7.1), the variable Y_i records the outcome for each participant. T_i is the assigned treatment for each participant. For treated participants, $T_i = 1$; for untreated participants, $T_i = 0$. Both Y_i and T_i are observed in the dataset that we will be working with. The variable U_i, by contrast, is unobserved and represents all of the remaining causes of Y_i. In other words, the regression equation characterizes Y_i as a combination of observed factors (in this case T_i) and unobserved factors (U_i).

The coefficients in this equation are the intercept a and the slope b. Here a represents the average outcome that we would observe if all observations were untreated.[1]

---

[1] This characterization of a implicitly assumes that the average value of U_i is zero. This assumption makes sense in the context of a randomized experiment, since the subjects assigned to the control group ($T_i = 0$) are a random sample of all subjects. Thus, the average outcome in the control group should be an unbiased estimator of the average untreated potential outcomes among all subjects.

More important for researchers is the coefficient b, which represents the average treatment effect (i.e., the average change in outcomes that would occur if all observations were moved from untreated to treated). As in previous chapters, estimating the ATE is our primary aim.

Least Squares Estimation: How does regression estimate the coefficients a and b? To answer this question, we first need to define a *residual*. Call $\widehat{a}$ the guess of a, and call $\widehat{b}$ the guess of b. If one were to predict Y_i based on these guesses, the prediction equation would be:

$$\text{Predicted value of } Y_i = \widehat{a} + \widehat{b}T_i. \tag{7.2}$$

A residual is the difference between the actual value of Y_i and the predicted value of Y_i:

$$\text{Residual} = Y_i - \left(\widehat{a} + \widehat{b}T_i \right). \tag{7.3}$$

A residual is greater than zero if a participant's observed outcome is greater than its predicted outcome. A residual is less than zero if the observed outcome is less than its predicted outcome. If a prediction is perfect, such that the predicted value of Y_i coincides exactly with the actual value of Y_i, the residual is zero.

Regression attempts to pick $\widehat{a}$ and $\widehat{b}$ so as to make the collection of residuals as small as possible. Since residuals may be positive or negative, regression calculates the square of each subject's residual so that small numbers represent better predictions. Regression selects the values of $\widehat{a}$ and $\widehat{b}$ that minimize the sum of the squared residuals for all participants, which is why regression is also called "least squares regression." (See Box 7.2 for a numeric example of how the sum of squared residuals is calculated.)

Regression and Difference-in-Means Estimation: One convenient feature of regression is that it exactly reproduces difference-in-means estimation when the treatment is the sole predictor of Y_i. In other words, the estimate $\widehat{b}$ produced by regression is the same number that one would obtain by subtracting the control group mean from the treatment group mean.

To illustrate the equivalence, let's revisit the Murrar and Brauer (2018) experiment described in Chapter 4. The treatment is scored $T_i = 1$ if subjects watched the sitcom *Little*

Box 7.2 Fitting a Regression Line by Minimizing the Sum of Squared Residuals

Building on the example in Box 7.1, suppose we use regression to estimate the intercept (a) and slope (b) in the equation:

$$Y_i = a + bT_i + U_i. \tag{7.4}$$

Regression calculates $\widehat{a}$ to be 3 and $\widehat{b}$ to be 4. Thus, the predicted values of Y_i may be obtained using the fitted line formula $3 + 4T_i$. Table 7.1 shows the residual for each participant. The sum of the squared residuals is 8. Regression selects the values of $\widehat{a}$ and $\widehat{b}$ so as to make the sum of squared residuals as small as possible. (Try some other values of $\widehat{a}$ and $\widehat{b}$, and you will find that the implied residuals have a larger sum of squares.) Notice that the regression estimate of the average treatment effect is the same as the difference-in-means estimate, since the mean in the control group is 3 and the mean in the treatment group is 7.

TABLE 7.1. *Illustration of how residuals are calculated*

Outcome (Y_i)	Treatment (T_i)	$\widehat{a}$	$\widehat{b}$	$\widehat{a} + \widehat{b}T_i$	Residual	Squared Residual
2	0	3	4	3	−1	1
4	0	3	4	3	1	1
3	0	3	4	3	0	0
5	1	3	4	7	−2	4
8	1	3	4	7	1	1
8	1	3	4	7	1	1

Mosque on the Prairie and $T_i = 0$ if subjects watched the sitcom *Friends*. The experiment had many outcome measures; for this example, we will focus on how warmly participants rated Arabs on a scale from 0 to 100 shortly after viewing the sitcoms.

```
murrar$Y <- murrar$arab_t1
murrar$T <- murrar$condition
```

One way to instruct R to compute means in the control and treatment groups is to use the `tapply` command:

```
> tapply(murrar$Y, murrar$T, mean, na.rm = TRUE)
        0        1
64.15730 70.52326
```

The difference-in-means is therefore 6.36596. When we use R to regress Y_i on the treatment T_i, we reproduce this estimate:

```
> summary(lm(Y ~ T, data = murrar))

Coefficients:
            Estimate Std. Error t value Pr(>|t|)
(Intercept)   64.157      2.139  29.990   <2e-16 ***
T              6.366      3.052   2.086   0.0384 *
---
Signif. codes:  0 `***' 0.001 `**' 0.01 `*' 0.05 `.' 0.1 ` ' 1

Residual standard error: 20.18 on 173 degrees of freedom
  (18 observations deleted due to missingness)
Multiple R-squared:  0.02454,   Adjusted R-squared:  0.0189
F-statistic: 4.352 on 1 and 173 DF,  p-value: 0.03844
```

Difference-in-means and regression both render an estimated ATE of 6.366, and the regression estimate for the intercept (64.157) is the same as the mean of the control group.

Visualizing a Fitted Regression Line: In order to get an intuitive sense of how the regression results emerge from the raw outcomes, researchers often superimpose a *fitted regression line* ($\widehat{a} + \widehat{b}T_i$) on a plot of T_i and Y_i. Figure 7.1 places T_i on the horizontal axis and Y_i on the vertical axis. This plot is similar to the individual values plot shown in Figure 3.3, except now a line with an intercept $\widehat{a}$ and slope $\widehat{b}$ connects the control group

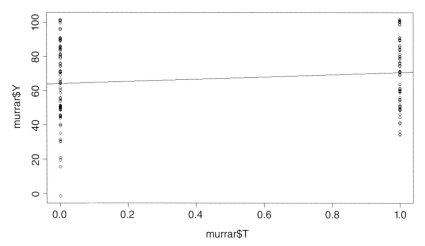

FIGURE 7.1. Scatterplot of Y (warmth toward Arabs) and T (assigned sitcom), with a fitted regression line

mean to the treatment group mean.[2] Slope refers to the vertical change that occurs with a one-unit shift along the horizontal axis. In this case, a one-unit shift along the horizontal axis (from $T = 0$ to $T = 1$) coincides with a 6.366 rise in average outcomes, which is the estimated average treatment effect. The residuals are the vertical distances between each of the points and the regression line. Points below the fitted regression line have negative residuals; those above the line have positive residuals.

Regression Adjustment: Regression is often used to analyze experimental data because it can "adjust" for covariates in ways that may improve the precision with which the ATE is estimated. Adjustment does two things: it removes the correlation between each covariate and the outcome, and it removes the correlation between each covariate and the treatment. After adjustment, what remains is the "unique" part of Y_i that is uncorrelated with the covariates and the unique part of T_i that is uncorrelated with the covariates.

Why would we be interested in the unique parts of Y_i and T_i? The unique part of Y_i may be more informative than the original Y_i because its standard deviation is smaller. (Recall from Chapter 3 that, all else being equal, the standard error diminishes with the standard deviation of the outcome.) The unique part of Y_i excludes variation stemming from the fact that the participants have different background attributes that are correlated with outcomes. It may be helpful to think of the unique part of Y_i as what we would have observed had all the participants entered the experiment with the same background attributes as the average participant. The unique part of T_i is useful because it eliminates any chance imbalance in background attributes that may have occurred when random assignment placed participants in one experimental group rather than the other. The unique component of T_i isolates the treatment versus control comparison by removing any part of T_i that could have been predicted by background attributes.

---

[2] A small amount of vertical jitter has been added to the points to make them visible when multiple points occupy the same location.

Expanding a regression model to adjust for pre-treatment covariates is straightforward. For example, in the *Little Mosque* experiment, the researchers measured warmth toward Arabs and warmth toward Whites before subjects were exposed to the treatment or control videos. Both ratings ranged from 0 to 100. Let's call each participant's baseline rating of Arabs A_i and baseline rating of Whites W_i. The expanded regression equation is now:

$$Y_i = a + bT_i + cA_i + dW_i + U_i'. \tag{7.5}$$

Our aim is still to estimate b, the average treatment effect, but now regression will generate guesses of four parameters (a, b, c, d) when minimizing the sum of squared residuals. The term U_i' refers to the set of omitted causes of Y_i. Unlike U_i, the unobserved term U_i' does not include A_i or W_i, which are no longer omitted from the regression model.

Are these covariates likely to improve the precision with which the ATE is estimated? The gains from covariate adjustment boil down to whether the included covariates successfully predict Y_i (i.e., reduce the sum of squared residuals). The more accurately the covariates predict Y_i, the more valuable they are.[3] In the *Little Mosque* example, intuition suggests that the covariates will be predictive because the baseline measures are similar in substance and format to the outcome measure. The warmth rating of Arabs (A_i) expressed shortly before viewing the sitcoms should be correlated with the warmth rating of Arabs (Y_i) expressed shortly after viewing. The pre-treatment warmth rating of Whites may also be correlated with Y_i if certain subjects tend to give warm (or cold) ratings to all groups.

Before instructing R to include covariates in the regression model, check whether the covariates include missing values. If so, replace the missing values with the mean of the non-missing values so that the number of observations remains the same in both the unadjusted and adjusted regressions. The R code here first calculates mean outcomes for the non-missing observations:

```
murrar$A <- murrar$arab_t0
murrar$W <- murrar$white_t0
avg.A <- mean(murrar$A, na.rm = TRUE)
avg.W <- mean(murrar$W, na.rm = TRUE)
```

The `ifelse()` function looks for missing data. When a missing value is found, the function inserts the means in its place:

```
murrar$A <- ifelse(is.na(murrar$A), avg.A, murrar$A)
murrar$W <- ifelse(is.na(murrar$W), avg.W, murrar$W)
```

With the covariates ready for inclusion, we add them to the regression equation:

```
> summary(lm(Y ~ T + A + W , data = murrar))
```

---

[3] Notice that the pre-treatment covariates need not *cause* Y_i. Covariates aid precision so long as they are correlated with Y_i, for whatever reason.

```
Coefficients:
            Estimate Std. Error t value Pr(>|t|)
(Intercept)  7.91433    3.48528   2.271 0.024407 *
T            5.71666    1.60769   3.556 0.000487 ***
A            0.79824    0.05242  15.228  < 2e-16 ***
W            0.06882    0.05680   1.212 0.227346
---
Signif. codes:  0 '***' 0.001 '**' 0.01 '*' 0.05 '.' 0.1 ' ' 1

Residual standard error: 10.59 on 171 degrees of freedom
  (18 observations deleted due to missingness)
Multiple R-squared:  0.7344,    Adjusted R-squared:  0.7297
F-statistic: 157.6 on 3 and 171 DF,  p-value: < 2.2e-16
```

Earlier, regression based on Eq. (7.1) estimated the average treatment effect to be 6.366 and its standard error to be 3.052. By comparison, the covariate-adjusted regression (based on Eq. (7.5)) estimates the ATE to be 5.717 with a standard error of just 1.608.

The change in the estimated ATE reflects the fact that the covariates were correlated with the assigned treatment. Typically, estimates of b do not change appreciably when covariates are added to the regression model, but they may increase or decrease. In this case, the covariate adjusted estimate is slightly lower than the unadjusted estimate.

To assess whether covariate adjustment yields a more precise estimate of the ATE, we examine the estimated standard errors. In this example, the change in the estimated standard error is considerable. Before adjustment, the standard error was estimated to be 3.052; after adjustment, the estimated standard error is 1.608.

In order to appreciate the improvement in precision, it is helpful to think about how much larger the number of subjects would have to be in order to achieve comparable precision without covariate adjustment. Recall that, all else being equal, the standard error declines with the square root of N. By adjusting for two covariates, regression increases the effective N in this study from 175 to approximately $175*(3.052/1.608)^2 = 630$. In other words, the covariate-adjusted standard errors are approximately the same as what the unadjusted standard errors would have been had the study comprised 630 participants instead of 175. The fact that Murrar and Brauer gathered covariate information during their base interview saved them the expense of having 455 more subjects watch sitcoms and fill out surveys.

Visualizing the Covariate-Adjusted Estimator of b: In order to visualize the fitted regression line after covariate adjustment, one superimposes the new line over a plot of the *unique* components of Y_i and T_i. The following steps describe the process of obtaining each unique component and the fitted regression line. The first two steps isolate the unique part of the treatment. Steps 3 and 4 isolate the unique part of the outcome. Steps 5 and 6 prepare the graph that illustrates how the estimated ATE emerged from the data. The R code may be found in the online appendix and the *R Companion*.

1. Regress T_i on the covariates.
2. Use the coefficients from this regression to calculate residuals. Call these residuals T_{resid}, which represents the part of T_i that is not predicted by the covariates.
3. Regress Y_i on the covariates.

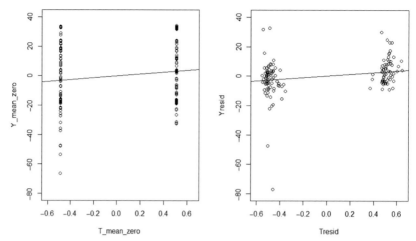

FIGURE 7.2. Visualizing the estimated ATE, without covariate adjustment (left panel) and with covariate adjustment (right panel)

4. Use the coefficients from this regression to calculate residuals. Call these residuals Y_{resid}, which represents the part of Y_i that is not predicted by the covariates.
5. To obtain the covariate-adjusted $\hat{b}$, regress Y_{resid} on T_{resid}.
6. Create a scatterplot of T_{resid} (horizontal axis) and Y_{resid} (vertical axis). Superimpose a fitted regression line using $\hat{a} + \hat{b} T_{resid}$ from step 5.

This graph is presented in the right panel of Figure 7.2. To illustrate the consequences of covariate adjustment, the left panel of Figure 7.2 shows an analogous plot from a regression of Y_i on T_i alone. To make it easy to compare the two graphs, I recentered Figure 7.1 so that the mean of Y_i is zero and the mean of T_i is zero. Apart from recentering, the left panel of Figure 7.2 is the same as Figure 7.1.

Comparing the covariate-adjusted plot to the unadjusted plot reveals three important differences. First, the horizontal location of the points differs after extracting the unique component of the treatment. Before covariate adjustment, the points in the control group are all at one value (−0.492) and the points in the treatment group are all at another value (0.508). In other words, the treatment and control observations are separated by exactly one unit along the horizontal axis. After adjustment, the values of T_{resid} are no longer identical for each member of the control group. Some T_{resid} values in the control group are especially low because their T_i scores were less than predicted by the covariates, and some T_{resid} values in the control group are especially high because their T_i scores were greater than predicted by the covariates. The same source of dispersion applies also to the treatment group. The T_{resid} values resemble clouds over the horizontal axis, whereas the T_i values look like vertical slabs.

The second difference is that the distribution of outcomes is much more compactly distributed along the vertical axis once we extract the unique component of the outcome. Whereas the standard deviation of Y_i is 20.4, the standard deviation of Y_{resid} is just 10.9. Because the Y_i values in each experimental group are bunched more closely together, the data points now provide more guidance about where the fitted regression line belongs. If you saw only a scatterplot of Y_{resid} and T_{resid}, you probably could draw a line by eye through the points that would come fairly close to the fitted regression line shown in the right panel of Figure 7.2.

A final difference between the two graphs is the location of the fitted regression line. Before covariate adjustment, the slope of the fitted regression line is just the difference-in-means (6.37). After covariate adjustment, the estimated slope (5.72) is slightly different because regression minimizes the sum of squared residuals with respect to T_{resid} rather than T_i.

Can Covariate Adjustment Ever Decrease Precision? Although covariate adjustment often improves precision, its benefits depend on the correlation between the covariates and the outcome. One or more covariates that are weakly correlated with Y_i will not reduce the sum of squared residuals appreciably. As a result, the standard deviation of Y_{resid} will be about the same as the standard deviation of Y_i, yielding little reduction in standard error. Meanwhile, covariate adjustment comes at a cost. One downside is the loss of *degrees of freedom*, the number of data points that are available to estimate the coefficients in the regression model. As more coefficients are estimated, less information remains to estimate the ATE. (The number of observations is the upper limit on how many coefficients can be estimated, but typically researchers stop well short of that ceiling.) Another downside is the incidental correlation that may exist between the covariates and the treatment. Recall that covariate adjustment isolates the unique component of the treatment T_i. However, as the standard deviation of T_{resid} declines, the standard error of the ATE increases. Adjusting for covariates that are uncorrelated with Y_i could, in principle, decrease the precision with which the ATE is estimated.

Whether the precision benefits outweigh precision losses depends on the particular application. A useful illustration of ineffective covariate adjustment may again be found in the `murrar` dataset. One of their outcome variables is a reaction time measure that assesses respondents' "implicit" attitudes toward Arabs as opposed to Whites. Let's call this implicit association test Y_i^{IAT}.

```
murrar$Y_IAT <- murrar$iatT1N
```

Using regression to estimate the effect of the treatment on this outcome without covariate adjustment, we obtain:

```
> summary(lm(Y_IAT ~ T, data = murrar))

Coefficients:
            Estimate Std. Error t value Pr(>|t|)
(Intercept)  0.07289    0.04438   1.642   0.1022
T           -0.17456    0.06226  -2.804   0.0056 **
---
Signif. codes:  0 '***' 0.001 '**' 0.01 '*' 0.05 '.' 0.1 ' ' 1

Residual standard error: 0.4233 on 183 degrees of freedom
  (8 observations deleted due to missingness)
Multiple R-squared:  0.04119,    Adjusted R-squared:  0.03595
F-statistic: 7.861 on 1 and 183 DF,  p-value: 0.005597
```

Because implicit attitudes were not measured in the baseline survey, they are not available as covariates. Suppose we include as covariates the same two attitude measures that we included earlier, warmth toward Arabs and warmth toward Whites. This regression produces the following output:

```
> summary(lm(Y_IAT ~ T + A + W, data = murrar))

Coefficients:
              Estimate Std. Error t value Pr(>|t|)
(Intercept)   0.041306   0.138202   0.299  0.76538
T            -0.173157   0.062586  -2.767  0.00625 **
A            -0.001021   0.002049  -0.499  0.61871
W             0.001271   0.002224   0.572  0.56831
---
Signif. codes:  0 '***' 0.001 '**' 0.01 '*' 0.05 '.' 0.1 ' ' 1

Residual standard error: 0.4253 on 181 degrees of freedom
  (8 observations deleted due to missingness)
Multiple R-squared:  0.04306,    Adjusted R-squared:  0.0272
F-statistic: 2.715 on 3 and 181 DF,  p-value: 0.04625
```

Covariate adjustment scarcely changes the estimated ATE and its estimated standard error. The two covariates are so weakly correlated with Y_i that they do little to reduce the sum of squared residuals (32.8 without covariates and 32.7 with covariates). Meanwhile, including these two covariates burns two degrees of freedom and scarcely reduces the standard deviation remaining in T_{resid}. In this case, there appear to be no precision gains from covariate adjustment.

7.2 ASSESSING SUBSTANTIVE AND STATISTICAL SIGNIFICANCE

What criteria should one use to assess whether the estimated average treatment effect is important? No clear consensus exists on this issue, perhaps reflecting the diverse scientific and practical objectives that motivate experimental research. What follows is a brief overview of the kinds of considerations that are often expressed by authors and critics when discussing the importance of research findings.

> *Are the results illuminating given prior research?* The answer is almost certainly yes if this study is the first experiment to address a particular research question. If this study addresses an established body of research, have previous findings come to a consensus about the effectiveness of the intervention, or does the new study speak to an active controversy? Does this study extend the research frontier in some way, by considering new interventions, understudied types of participants or contexts, or innovative outcome measures? Studies that replicate existing research can still be illuminating, especially if they are conducted in ways that estimate the ATE with precision.

Can the apparent ATE be converted into units that help convey its substantive importance? For example, if an intervention is designed to prevent deforestation, how many acres could be preserved through a nationwide rollout of the program? Because readers may not have a sense of whether this acreage figure is large or small, comparative benchmarks may be helpful. How does that acreage compare to the annual amount of forest loss in the region? Alternatively, one could compare the ATE to the range of variation that one typically observes in the absence of treatment. In this case, how large is the average treatment effect compared to the standard deviation of forest loss among control villages?

How effective is this intervention compared to others? Comparisons among interventions could focus on their relative costs or ease of implementation. For example, preventing deforestation by shoring up property rights requires government to implement and enforce legal titles; are there less expensive alternatives that are just as effective? Another way to compare interventions is to measure their effects on an array of outcomes. Do some interventions have especially long-lasting effects? Do some interventions have beneficial spillover effects?

Researchers should not feel obligated to argue that the interventions they studied are path-breaking or have profound policy implications. The aim is not to sell the interventions but rather to offer an evenhanded assessment of what has been learned.

The assessment of *statistical significance* is quite different from the assessment of substantive importance. Significance testing is a statistical procedure consisting of four steps.

Step 1: Formulate a *null hypothesis*. In the context of experimental research, the null hypothesis often takes the form, "The intervention has no average effect on participants' outcomes."

Step 2: Formulate an *alternative hypothesis*. By default, statistical software presumes that the alternative is that the average treatment effect is different from zero.[4]

Step 3: Define a *test statistic*, a number that reflects the size of the apparent treatment effect. One test statistic with attractive statistical properties is the so-called *t*-ratio, which is simply the estimated ATE divided by its estimated standard error. This statistic is routinely reported by regression packages. For example, looking back on the regression results we initially obtained when thermometer ratings of Arabs were regressed on treatment, we see that the *t*-ratio is 2.086.

Step 4: Calculate the *p*-value, or probability of obtaining a test statistic at least as large in absolute value as the one obtained from the experiment. In the Murrar and Brauer experiment, the *p*-value is the probability of obtaining a test statistic as large in absolute value as 2.086 simply by chance if the ATE were truly zero. In other words,

---

[4] This kind of alternative hypothesis is sometimes called a *two-tailed* alternative, because either large positive or large negative estimates would reject the null hypothesis. Another important class of alternative hypotheses are one-tailed, in that they specify that the treatment effect will produce change in a particular direction. For example, the *Little Mosque* intervention was presumed to increase warmth toward Arabs. When testing one-tailed hypotheses, the relevant *p*-values are half as large as the two-tailed *p*-values that regression reports by default. One-tailed tests are therefore "easier" in the sense that a *t*-ratio that falls short of significance using a two-tailed test might be deemed significant using a one-tailed test. To guard against the temptation to specify a one-tailed test after seeing the results, the direction of a one-tailed test should be specified in a pre-analysis plan before results are known.

Box 7.3 Assumptions Underlying the t-Test

R's regression package calculates *p*-values by comparing a test statistic to a reference distribution. The test statistic is the *t*-ratio, which is the estimated ATE divided by its estimated standard error. The reference distribution is known as the *t*-distribution; the precise contours of this bell-shaped distribution depend on the number of degrees of freedom, which is the number of participants minus the number of coefficients that the regression estimates. When the analysis involves more than 120 degrees of freedom, the *t*-distribution becomes indistinguishable from the familiar normal distribution.

For example, in the Murrar and Brauer experiment, regression without covariate adjustment produced an estimated ATE of 6.365952 with a standard error of 3.051638. Since 6.365952/3.051638 = 2.09, we instruct R to look up the probability of drawing a number as large (in absolute value) as 2.09 from a *t*-distribution with 173 degrees of freedom.

```
> 2*pt(-abs(2.09),173)
[1] 0.03808008
```

The answer is that 3.8 percent of such draws will yield numbers larger than 2.09 or less than −2.09, so the *p*-value is 0.038. If we had instructed R to conduct a one-tailed test on the grounds that the researchers expected *Little Mosque* to increase warmth toward Arab Muslims, the *p*-value would have been halved:

```
> pt(-abs(2.09),173)
[1] 0.01904004
```

How do we know that the *t*-distribution properly describes the sampling distribution of the estimated ATE? The use of the *t*-distribution in experiments with small numbers of participants is justified when the outcome is distributed normally. Simulation studies show that the *t*-distribution performs reasonably well even when the outcome is not normally distributed, so long as the distribution is distributed symmetrically (Sawilowsky and Blair 1992). When applied to outcomes with a skewed distribution (e.g., fundraising experiments, whose outcomes contain a large share of small contributions along with a handful of very large values), the *t*-distribution may produce inaccurate *p*-values. See Lachin (2020) for alternatives to the *t*-test when outcomes are skewed.

---

if the null hypothesis were true, could we have obtained a test statistic as large as 2.086 or as small as −2.086 by chance due to the way in which random assignment happened to allocate participants to treatment and control conditions? Invoking the assumptions described in Box 7.3, regression calculates this probability to be 0.038. This *p*-value means that if the treatment effect were truly zero and we were to replicate this experiment many times under identical conditions, only 3.8 percent of these hypothetical experiments would generate a test statistic as large as 2.086 or as small as −2.086. When this probability is below 5 percent, by convention the estimated ATE is declared to be "statistically significant." After covariate adjustment, the *t*-ratio grows to 3.556, and regression declares this *p*-value to be "0.000." Since we do not see any further digits, this probability is written $p < 0.001$. Again, because this number is below 0.05, the estimated ATE would be deemed statistically significant. Both tests, but especially the second one, reject the null hypothesis on the grounds that if the ATE were truly zero, random assignment would rarely generate a test statistic as large (in absolute value) as we actually observe.

Hypothesis testing is an informative exercise, and it can be reassuring to know that one's experimental results would seldom occur by chance if the intervention truly had no effect on average. However, reflections on substantive importance are too often upstaged by the narrow question of whether the estimated average treatment effect is statistically significant. A statistically significant estimate need not be substantively meaningful. A large experiment might produce a small estimated ATE that achieves statistical significance because its estimated standard error is very small.

Conversely, one can imagine a small study that generates a substantively large estimate of the ATE. The results are intriguing, but the estimated ATE falls short of the usual standards of statistical significance because more than 5 percent of the hypothetical random assignments under the null hypothesis generate an estimated ATE at least as large as the intriguing estimate. This estimate is still our best guess of the ATE even if we remain uncertain. The last point deserves emphasis. One of the most common errors of interpretation is to infer that the ATE is zero because the experiment rendered a statistically insignificant estimate of the ATE. This distinction between a statistically insignificant estimate and an estimate of zero is illustrated in the exercises.

Dismissal of statistically insignificant findings sometimes reflects a deeper misconception. Those with a shallow appreciation for scientific inquiry will sometimes assert that the goal of experimental research is to find evidence of big treatment effects. According to this view, the bigger the apparent effect, the more important the experiment is. A moment's reflection reveals why this view is misguided. Suppose one wanted to assess the effects of a preposterous biomedical hypothesis, such as the notion that magical incantations prevent infectious disease. The objective of a well-designed experiment is to find the true average treatment effect, which in this case is zero. Finding a big treatment effect when none exists is an instance of failure, not success.

7.3 CONCLUSION

This closing chapter introduces topics that should prove useful as you work with data or read articles that report experimental findings. Regression is very widely used to analyze experiments. Regression provides a flexible way to adjust for covariates and, in so doing, improve the precision with which the ATE is estimated. The benefits of covariate adjustment depend on the available covariates, and one design implication is that researchers should be on the lookout for opportunities to measure covariates that are likely to predict outcomes. Indeed, when resources are tight, it may make sense to design an experiment around a pool of participants for which rich covariate data have already been gathered.

Another useful feature of regression is that it provides a helpful way to visualize the relationship between treatment and outcome. Superimposing a fitted regression line over a scatterplot provides an intuitive picture of how clearly the data suggest an average treatment effect. Updating this plot after covariate adjustment may help sharpen one's sense of the average treatment effect, especially if covariates expunge a good deal of extraneous variation in outcomes. The mechanics of regression and graphical representation of causal effects are two useful stepping stones to more advanced topics in experimental design. See, for example, Gerber and Green (2012) on the analysis of block randomized designs and Coppock (2021) on graphical tools for experimental data analysis.

Finally, we broached the topic of how one might assess and convey the importance of one's experimental findings. The main recommendation was to reflect on the ways in which a given experiment contributes to existing knowledge. In what ways is the study at hand innovative or distinctive? What do its results imply for theory, practice, or research design? This discussion of importance helps put into proper perspective the topic of significance testing, which focuses on whether the results at hand could plausibly be attributed to chance if there were truly no average treatment effect. Addressing this skeptical conjecture is an instructive exercise and provides a stepping stone to more advanced hypothesis tests focusing on the empirical sustainability of core assumptions. See Gerber and Green (2012), for example, on the use of hypothesis testing to assess whether attrition has jeopardized the core assumption of random assignment. At the same time, our discussion of significance testing sought to call attention to the distinction between statistical significance and substantive importance. A substantively important research finding that falls short of statistical significance calls out for further investigation. A statistically significant research finding that is substantively unimportant does not.

EXERCISES

The datasets used in the exercises are available from the book's webpage: https://osf.io/b78je/, or you may import them directly into R by installing the package `experimentr`.

7.1 Using the `murrar` dataset, show that the correspondence between regression and difference-in-means holds when T_i is scored 0 for control and 1 for treatment, but that it no longer holds if T_i were scored −1 for control and 1 for treatment.

7.2 Lynn and Mynier (1993) report the results of two experiments that test whether the "posture" of restaurant waitstaff affects the tips they receive. Study 2 took place at a Chinese restaurant over a two-week period and involved 148 distinct sets of customers. The authors explain that "When visiting a table for the first time, the waitress would greet her customers, introduce herself by name, ask how the customers were doing, and take the customers' drink orders. These tasks were performed either in a standing or squatting position depending on the outcome of the coin toss" (p. 681). The outcome is the size of the tip (in dollars) for each table. The covariates are the number of customers dining at each table, the amount of the bill, whether the bill was paid by credit card, whether the waitress' shift was during the day or evening, and whether the bill was paid by a man or woman.

  a. Write a regression model in which tip is the outcome and crouch is the treatment. Estimate the average treatment effect and its standard error using the `lynn` dataset.

  b. Before adding covariates to this regression, first consider whether they are truly "pre-treatment"; for each one, discuss whether the covariate could be affected by the treatment.

c. Augment the regression model in part (a) with any covariates that you deem to be unaffected by treatment. Be sure that the covariates do not include any missing values. If a variable's observations would be dropped due to missing values, replace them with the means of the non-missing values for that variable. Estimate the ATE and its standard error.

d. Graph the unadjusted and adjusted estimates of the ATE. Explain how covariate adjustment affects the slope and the precision with which it is estimated.

e. Does the estimated ATE in part (c) suggest that the crouching effect is substantively important? Why or why not?

f. Test the null hypothesis that crouching has no effect on tips using the two-tailed test provided in R's regression output. Is the crouching effect statistically significant? What does that mean?

7.3 Recall from Chapter 4 that Frijters et al. (2019) assess the extent to which college students' body mass index (BMI) is affected by their roommates' BMI. Roommates were randomly assigned. The dataset `frijters` contains each student's current BMI (`Current_BMI`), their BMI at baseline (`Past_BMI`), and the average of their roommates' BMI at baseline (`Roommate_BMI`). In contrast to most of the examples we have discussed, this one features a "treatment" that is continuous, reflecting the average BMI of the randomly assigned roommates.

a. A regression equation expresses the outcome (`Current_BMI`) as a function of a treatment (`Roommate_BMI`) and an unobserved error term (U_i):

$$\text{Current\_BMI} = a + b(\text{Roommate\_BMI}) + U_i.$$

Use regression to estimate the coefficients, a and b. The slope b is of particular interest, as it indicates the rate at which `Current_BMI` changes, on average, due to a one-unit change in `Roommate_BMI`. Interpret regression's estimate of the slope b.

b. Using this fitted regression equation, predict a student's `Current_BMI` when `Roommate_BMI` is 14.5 (the lowest value in this dataset). Next, predict a student's `Current_BMI` when `Roommate_BMI` is 34.4 (the highest value in this dataset).

c. How do the estimate of b and its estimated standard error change when you expand the regression equation to adjust for `Past_BMI`?

7.4 Regression can be used to estimate treatment effects when an experiment features more than one treatment arm. Recall from Chapter 4 that the survey experiment conducted by Mullinix et al. (2021) presented online respondents with text-only, video-only, or text-plus-video descriptions of actual instances of police use of force resulting in death or injury. The data may be found in `mullinix`. When working with this dataset, be aware of the fact that some variables contain missing values (NA). You will have to tell R how you want it to handle missing values.

a. Focusing solely on the control group and the three treatment groups involving the lethal use of force, calculate average responses for each experimental group to the question, "To what extent do you approve or disapprove of the way the police in the United States are doing their job?" (1 = strongly disapprove,

7 = strongly approve). Use difference-in-means to calculate the three treatment effects by comparing each treatment group's mean to the control group's mean.

b. Show that regression can be used to reproduce these results. Create an indicator for the first treatment, scored 1 if respondents were exposed to the first treatment and 0 otherwise. Create an indicator for the second treatment, scored 1 if respondents were exposed to the second treatment and 0 otherwise. Create an indicator for the third treatment, scored 1 if respondents were exposed to the third treatment and 0 otherwise. Write down a regression model that expresses the outcome as a function of all three of these indicator variables. Estimate the coefficients of this model, and confirm that they reproduce the difference-in-means estimates that you calculated in part (a).

7.5 Some insights about research design can be gleaned from the formula that regression uses to estimate the standard errors of the ATE. Again, we use the Murrar and Brauer (1998) experiment as an illustration. Before covariate adjustment, the formula for the estimated standard error of the ATE is:

$$\sqrt{\frac{\dfrac{Sum\ of\ Squared\ Residuals}{(N-k)}}{(N-1)SD^2(T_i)}} = \sqrt{\frac{\dfrac{70463.2512}{(175-2)}}{(174)(0.2513629)}} = 3.051638,$$

where N is the number of participants, k is the number of coefficients to be estimated, and $SD^2(T_i)$ is the squared standard deviation of T_i.

After covariate adjustment, the formula for the estimated standard error of the ATE is:

$$\sqrt{\frac{\dfrac{Sum\ of\ Squared\ Residuals}{(N-k)}}{(N-1)SD^2(T_{resid})}} = \sqrt{\frac{\dfrac{19185.2324}{(175-4)}}{(174)(0.2494706)}} = 1.607686,$$

where, again, $SD^2(T_{resid})$ is the squared standard deviation of T_{resid}.

a. All else being equal, as the sum of squared residuals increases, does the estimated standard error increase or decrease?

b. All else being equal, as k increases, does the estimated standard error increase or decrease?

c. Notice that, with covariance adjustment, the standard deviation of T_{resid} is smaller than the standard deviation of T_i because T_{resid} contains only the unique component of T_i that is unrelated to the covariates. Does this reduction in standard deviation increase or decrease the estimated standard error of the estimated ATE?

d. To prevent a reduction in standard deviation in T_i due to covariate adjustment, some researchers conduct "blocked" randomization. Blocks of participants with similar covariate profiles are assembled, and exactly half of the participants in each block are placed into the treatment group. This procedure ensures that the resulting randomization produces treatment and control groups with nearly identical covariate profiles. Because T_i is uncorrelated with these covariates, T_i and T_{resid} have the same standard deviation. In this experiment, what would the estimated standard error have been after covariate adjustment had the standard deviation of T_{resid} been the same as the standard deviation of T_i?

7.6 When reading regression results, scholars sometimes interpret statistically insignificant estimates as though they were zero. In order to appreciate the distinction between an estimate of zero and a nonzero estimate that falls short of significance, consider the following example. Suppose you conduct an experiment involving 300 participants. However, before you know anything about the results, you receive data for a random selection of 150 participants; data for the other 150 participants remain undisclosed. Based on the 150 participants whose results are available to you, you estimate the ATE to be 5 with a standard error of 4. The two-tailed *p*-value is 0.21, so the estimated ATE is deemed to be nonsignificant.

   a. With this information in mind, think about what you expect to find when you analyze <u>only</u> the 150 as-yet undisclosed observations. If you were to place a bet, would you say the estimated ATE for this group of participants is more likely to be positive than negative, more likely to be negative than positive, or equally likely to be positive or negative?

   b. How would your answer to part (a) change if the first 150 observations had produced an estimated ATE of 0 with a standard error of 4?

7.7 Suppose you were hired to assess the Murrar and Brauer (2018) findings by a public agency that sought to reduce Canadians' hostility toward Arab immigrants. Using the data from their study, address the following questions.

   a. How important are the effects of exposure to *Little Mosque* on participants' ratings of warmth toward Arabs immediately after viewing the sitcom? How large is the estimated ATE in relation to the standard deviation in the control group?

   b. Does the fact that the program was aired to large audiences increase the importance you attach to the apparent effect of the treatment? Why or why not?

   c. How does your assessment of importance change in light of the follow-up interviews, which measured warmth toward Arabs a few weeks later? Are the estimated effects obtained from the follow-up interview statistically significant? If yes/no, what do you infer?

Solutions to Exercises

The datasets used in the end-of-chapter exercises may be found in the R library called `experimentr`. The R output shown in the solutions here has been edited so that it fits more compactly on the page. Complete code and output may be found in the online appendix (https://osf.io/b78je/).

CHAPTER 2

2.1 a. In the civil versus uncivil comparison, the group treated with uncivil discourse and the "baseline" group exposed to civil discourse watch a debate between political candidates. In this case, the average treatment effect (ATE) represents the average effect of exposure to debates with different levels of civility. Comparing the untreated control group to the treatment group exposed to uncivil dialogue, on the other hand, captures both the effect of watching a political debate (regardless of civility) *and* the effect of uncivil discourse.

   b. Using actors to portray civil or uncivil political candidates creates a more salient portrayal of uncivil discourse, and the tone and content of the discourse can be controlled by the experimenter so that the civil and uncivil debates are otherwise similar in content. The use of actors has advantages and disadvantages. The actors' portrayal can be a realistic example of incivility that prompts a response from participants. However, a scripted depiction by actors may not reflect incivility that typically occurs between politicians.

2.2 a. The subjects are the bill-paying customers at each table who receive the bills and decide on the amount to tip.

   b. Random assignment after the customers finish their meal ensures that other parts of the service during the meal are symmetrical and not affected by the random assignment. Suppose random assignment occurred when customers were first seated. If the waitstaff are induced by the assignment to smiley face condition to provide better service, then the difference in outcome between the treatment condition and the control condition may capture the difference in service as well as the addition of the smiley face, which would bias the estimated effect of the smiley face alone.

c. The experiment's design strives to maintain symmetry between the treatment and control groups. Once waitstaff deliver the bill to customers, the friendliness of their subsequent conversation could be affected by the smiley face in ways that could affect the tip. Preventing this type of interaction helps isolate the effect of the smiley face.

d. Using tips as the outcome measure creates a standard outcome that is unobtrusively measured and substantively meaningful (both to waitstaff and to customers). A survey could allow the researchers to gain greater insight and a more holistic understanding of the customer's response. However, it has disadvantages: It demands more time from customers, who may refuse to participate, and their responses may not have the same frankness as a monetary tip.

2.3 a. By comparing people who are assigned to the thank-you-for-voting condition to those in a reminder condition, the researcher holds constant the mention of the upcoming election and isolates the effect of the gratitude message.

b. By comparing thank-you-for-voting to no reminder, the researcher estimates the combined effect of a reminder and a message expressing gratitude. If this comparison were all that the researcher had to go on, an apparent positive effect would leave open the question of whether any reminder, even one without gratitude, would have increased turnout.

c. Comparing turnout rates among those who received a reminder mail versus control subjects, who received no mail, allows the researcher to estimate the ATE of the reminder on turnout. An estimate close to zero implies that reminders (that do not express gratitude) are ineffective.

2.4 In addition to the names that may communicate differences in race, the difference in the extracurricular activity also communicates details about the two high school applicants. The use of a Future Investment Banker Club compared to an African American Student Association introduces an extra piece of information that is not on Jamal Washington's application: An association with investment banking. This additional facet of the application may introduce other considerations for the participants; perhaps Arthur Wolfe is presumed to come from an affluent background and may not need a college scholarship. The intended comparison of otherwise identical Black and White applicants might in fact be a comparison of a putative Black applicant to an applicant who may be perceived as both White and affluent.

2.5 Each participant has two potential outcomes that correspond to what *would* happen if they were assigned to a treatment or control group. If they were assigned to the treatment group, the researcher would observe their treated outcome. If they were assigned to the control group, the researcher would observe their untreated outcome. Although each subject has more than one potential outcome, a subject actually expresses just one potential outcome, which is the observed outcome.

2.6 Each subject's treatment effect is the difference between the treated potential outcome and the control potential outcome. As it is not possible to observe both the treated potential outcome and the control potential outcome for any subject, researchers must set their sights on estimating the average treatment effect, which is the average difference between the treated potential outcomes and the untreated potential outcomes among all subjects.

2.7 Random assignment that gives each subject the same probability of being assigned to the treatment group will create a treatment group that has the same expected potential outcomes as the control group. Any given random assignment may produce control and treatment groups whose characteristics differ due to chance, but the use of random assignment ensures that the two groups have the same potential outcomes on average, over hypothetical replications of the assignment.

2.8 A sampling distribution is the collection of estimates from all possible random assignments. For example, the sampling distribution of the difference-in-means estimator of the ATE is the collection of difference-in-means estimates that we would obtain if we could perform every possible random assignment using a given experimental design.

2.9 The standard error is the standard deviation of the sampling distribution. The larger the standard error, the more dispersed the estimates are around the average estimate. Researchers strive for designs that will generate estimates that lie close to the ATE and therefore have a small standard error.

2.10 An estimator is a method or algorithm that is used to make an estimate. For example, the difference-in-means estimator guesses the value of the ATE by subtracting the average untreated outcome from the average treated outcome. An unbiased estimator is an algorithm that, on average, recovers the true parameter of interest, such as the ATE. The difference-in-means estimator, for example, is an unbiased estimator of the ATE when applied to a randomized experiment that satisfies the three core assumptions.

2.11 a. Treated Outcome $= (16 + 25)/2 = 20.5$
Untreated Outcome $= (12 + 29 + 18)/3 = 19.7$

$$\widehat{ATE} = 20.5 - 19.7 = 0.8$$

b. By calculating the estimated ATE for each of the five randomizations, we see that the average is equal to the true ATE, which reflects the fact that the difference-in-means estimator is unbiased.

Person in Treatment	Average Treated Outcome	Average Untreated Outcome	Estimated ATE
Abel	16	$(12 + 25 + 29 + 18)/4 = 21$	−5
Baker	20	$(11 + 25 + 29 + 18)/4 = 20.75$	−0.75
Charlie	25	$(11 + 12 + 29 + 18)/4 = 17.5$	7.5
Deborah	27	$(11 + 12 + 25 + 18)/4 = 16.5$	10.5
Elizabeth	22	$(11 + 12 + 25 + 29)/4 = 16.5$	2.75
		Average of Estimated ATE	3

c. The standard error for one of five subjects in treatment is larger than the standard error with two of five in treatment.

Standard error with 1/5 subjects in treatment:

$$\sqrt{\frac{(-5-3)^2 + (-0.75-3)^2 + (7.5-3)^2 + (10.5-3)^2 + (2.75-3)^2}{5}} = 5.56$$

Standard error with 2/5 subjects in treatment:

$$\sqrt{\frac{(-6-3)^2 + (-3-3)^2 + (-0.67-3)^2 + (0.83-3)^2 + (3.17-3)^2 + (3.17-3)^2 + (5.5-3)^2 + (6.17-3)^2 + (8.5-3)^2 + (12.33-3)^2}{10}} = 5.18$$

2.12 Unbiased inference requires random assignment (assignment to treatment or control that is independent of potential outcomes); noninterference (each subject's outcomes reflect only whether that subject is treated or not); and symmetry (the only experimentally-generated factor that differs between the treatment and control conditions is the treatment).

2.13 a. Consider the Balcells et al. (2022) experiment that studies the effect of a visit to the Museum of Memory and Human Rights on support for military rule. Random assignment was conducted for allocation of participants to the treatment or control condition. Attrition may jeopardize the randomization assumption, as some students dropped out of the experiment after assignment or did not respond to later survey requests so that their outcomes are not recorded. The students in the treatment and control groups who remain in the study after attrition may not have comparable potential outcomes.

　　The second assumption is noninterference. A threat to noninterference could include students in the treatment condition discussing the museum visit with students in the control condition.

　　Third, symmetry requires that the only systematic difference between the conditions be the treatment. One possible violation of this symmetry is the conditions under which the first post-treatment surveys were conducted. The control group completed their surveys in the school's computer lab whereas the treated participants took their surveys immediately after visiting the museum on their own cellphone or tablet devices.

b. Violation of the random assignment condition is the most concerning, especially as attrition rates climbed in long-term follow-up surveys. Attrition, especially if it causes different types of people to drop out of the study in each experimental group, can cause the treatment and control groups to no longer have potential outcomes that are similar in expectation, leading to biased estimates of the average treatment effect. The researchers took steps to minimize the likelihood of interference by limiting opportunities for participants' interaction. The symmetry assumption seems defensible for the follow-up surveys, as both treatment and control groups seemed to take the surveys in the same manner and at the same time.

2.14 Replicating a previously conducted experiment using a different set of participants serves two purposes. First, it expands the group of subjects in ways that might improve the precision with which the ATE is estimated. Second, replication allows us to understand whether the findings of the study are generalizable. Using a different group of participants expands our understanding of whether the initial study's results apply to different people and settings.

CHAPTER 3

3.1 The standard error can be estimated using the following equation:

$$\widehat{Standard\ Error} = \sqrt{\frac{Standard\ Deviation^2_{control}}{N_{control}} + \frac{Standard\ Deviation^2_{treatment}}{N_{treatment}}},$$

$$\widehat{Standard\ Error} = \sqrt{\frac{0.58^2}{15} + \frac{0.94^2}{15}} = 0.285.$$

The 95% confidence interval can be found using the following R code. The lower bound of the confidence interval is −0.834 and the upper bound is 0.334.

```
> t_multiplier <- qt(0.025, 28, lower.tail = FALSE)
> t_multiplier
[1]  2.048407
>
> lower_interval <- -0.25 - t_multiplier*0.285
> upper_interval <- -0.25 + t_multiplier*0.285
>
> cbind(lower_interval, upper_interval)
      lower_interval upper_interval
[1,]      -0.833796       0.333796
```

3.2 a. The means in the treatment and control groups:

```
> mean_treatment <- mean(poori$score[ poori$group == 1] )
> mean_treatment
[1]  11
>
> mean_control <- mean(poori$score[ poori$group == 0] )
> mean_control
[1]  8.533333
```

b. Standard deviations in the treatment and control groups:

```
> sd_treatment <- sd(poori$score[ poori$group == 1] )
> sd_treatment
[1]  2.236068
>
> sd_control <- sd(poori$score[ poori$group == 0] )
> sd_control
[1]  1.807392
```

c. Average treatment effect:

```
> mean_treatment - mean_control
[1]  2.466667
```

d. Standard error of the average treatment effect:

```
> n_treatment <- length(poori$group[ poori$group == 1])
> n_control <- length(poori$group[ poori$group == 0])
>
> standard_error <- sqrt(sd_control^2/n_control + sd_treatment^2/n_treatment)
> standard_error
[1] 0.7423686
```

e. Standard error if treatment group size were 60 and control group size were 30:

```
> n_control <- 30
> n_treatment <- 60
>
> standard_error <- sqrt(sd_control^2/n_control + sd_treatment^2/n_treatment)
> standard_error
[1] 0.4384315
```

3.3 Plot of YouTube experiment outcomes by treatment assignment, shown in Figure S.1:

```
> plot(x = youtube$group + rnorm(30, mean = 0, sd = .03), y = youtube$outcome,
+       main = "Outcomes by Experimental Group",
+       xlab = "Control = 0, Treatment = 1", ylab = "Outcome")
```

3.4 a. ATE and standard error using first measurement of bounce height:

```
> mean_treatment <- mean(batteries$one[ batteries$treatment == 1])
> mean_control <- mean(batteries$one[ batteries$treatment == 0])
>
> mean_treatment - mean_control
[1] 0.1246667
> sd_treatment <- sd(batteries$one[ batteries$treatment == 1])
> sd_control <- sd(batteries$one[ batteries$treatment == 0])
>
```

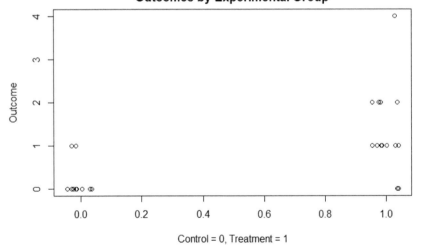

FIGURE S.1. Individual values plot of outcomes by assigned treatment

```
> n_treatment <- length(batteries$treatment[ batteries$treatment == 1])
> n_control <- length(batteries$treatment[ batteries$treatment == 0])
>
> standard_error <- sqrt(sd_control^2/n_control + sd_treatment^2/n_treatment)
> standard_error
[1] 0.01423833
```

b. ATE and standard error using average of three bounce heights:

```
> batteries$avg_bounce <- (batteries$one + batteries$two + batteries$three)/3
>
> mean_treatment <- mean(batteries$avg_bounce[ batteries$treatment == 1])
> mean_control <- mean(batteries$avg_bounce[ batteries$treatment == 0])
>
> mean_treatment - mean_control
[1] 0.1244444
> sd_treatment <- sd(batteries$avg_bounce[ batteries$treatment == 1])
> sd_control <- sd(batteries$avg_bounce[ batteries$treatment == 0])
>
> n_treatment <- length(batteries$treatment[ batteries$treatment == 1])
> n_control <- length(batteries$treatment[ batteries$treatment == 0])
>
> standard_error <- sqrt(sd_control^2/n_control + sd_treatment^2/n_treatment)
> standard_error
[1] 0.008948609
```

c. The standard error of the three-measurement average (0.009) is smaller than that of just the first measurement (0.014). The average of the three measurements has less variability, thus reducing the numerator of Eq. (3.1), which in turn reduces the standard error.

d. The plot of pretest bounce times compared to posttest bounce times shown in Figure S.2 does not reveal a clear pattern.

```
> plot(x = batteries$pre + rnorm(30, mean = 0, sd = .03), y = batteries$one,
+      main = "Pretest vs Posttest Bounce Time",
+      xlab = "Pretest", ylab = "Posttest")
```

e. When we use change scores in bounce time, we find that the precision implied by the standard error is the same as the standard error calculated using the posttest outcome alone.

```
> sd_treatment <- sd(batteries$diff[ batteries$treatment == 1])
> sd_control <- sd(batteries$diff[ batteries$treatment == 0])
>
> n_treatment <- length(batteries$treatment[ batteries$treatment == 1])
> n_control <- length(batteries$treatment[ batteries$treatment == 0])
>
> standard_error <- sqrt(sd_control^2/n_control + sd_treatment^2/n_treatment)
> standard_error
[1] 0.01451217
```

3.5 a. If one discards the damaged plants, one is effectively introducing a source of attrition, which could lead to bias if deer were attracted to plants that were enlarged due to the fertilizer. Better to measure all outcomes, including those from the damaged plants.

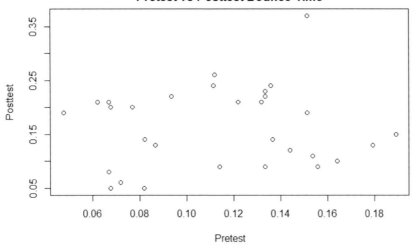

FIGURE S.2. Plot comparing pretest and posttest bounce times

b. Discarding the experiment and starting again in effect means estimating the effects of fertilizer only for instances where deer damage does not occur. That might be sensible if readers live in places where deer are not a concern. But in places where deer are abundant, one reason why it may be pointless to use fertilizer is that deer damage may undo any good that fertilizer does. In other words, deer are one of the many factors that shape the potential outcomes of plants.

CHAPTER 4

4.1 a. The plot shown in Figure S.3 depicts a positive correlation between pretest scores and posttest scores.

```
> plot(x = jitter(murrar$diff_t0), y = murrar$diff_t1,
+       main = "Pretest vs Posttest Difference Scores",
+       xlab = "Pretest", ylab = "Posttest")
```

b. The plot shown in Figure S.4 indicates that the treatment group has, on average, higher difference scores than the control group.

```
> plot(x = jitter(murrar$cond, 0.25), y = murrar$diff_t1,
+       main = "Treatment Assignment vs Posttest Difference Score",
+       xlab = "Treatment Assignment", ylab = "Posttest")
>
> clip(x1 = -0.1, x2 = 0.1, y1 = -20, y2 = 0)
> abline(h = mean(murrar$diff_t1[ murrar$cond == 0], na.rm = TRUE))
> clip(x1 = 0.9, x2 = 1.1, y1 = -20, y2 = 0)
> abline(h = mean(murrar$diff_t1[ murrar$cond == 1], na.rm = TRUE))
```

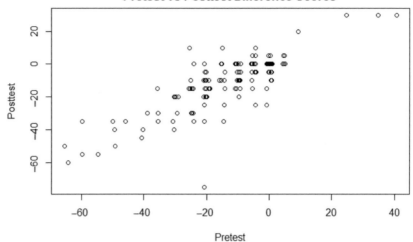

FIGURE S.3. Plot comparing pretest and posttest thermometer ratings

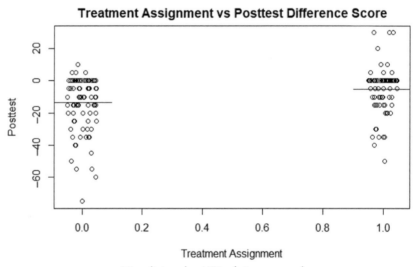

FIGURE S.4. Visualizing the ATE of sitcoms on change scores

c. The treatment (watching six episodes of the show *Little Mosque*) appears to have increased the posttest difference scores (of warmth toward Arabs compared to warmth toward Whites) by an average of 8.02 points over the control group's average difference score. The standard error is estimated to be 2.32. The interval ranging from 3.44 to 12.61 has a 95 percent chance of bracketing the average treatment effect; in other words, intervals formed in this manner will bracket the true ATE in 95 percent of the random assignments conducted under identical conditions.

```
> mean_treatment <- mean(murrar$diff_t1[ murrar$cond == 1], na.rm = TRUE)
> mean_control <- mean(murrar$diff_t1[ murrar$cond == 0], na.rm = TRUE)
>
> ate <- mean_treatment - mean_control
> ate
[ 1]  8.023909

> sd_treatment <- sd(murrar$diff_t1[ murrar$cond == 1], na.rm = TRUE)
> sd_control <- sd(murrar$diff_t1[ murrar$cond == 0], na.rm = TRUE)
>
> n_treatment <- nrow(murrar[ murrar$cond == 1 & !is.na(murrar$diff_t1), ])
> n_control <- nrow(murrar[ murrar$cond == 0 & !is.na(murrar$diff_t1), ])
>
> standard_error <- sqrt(sd_control^2/n_control + sd_treatment^2/n_treatment)
> standard_error
[ 1]  2.321479

> t_multiplier <- qt(0.025, (n_treatment + n_control - 2), lower.tail = FALSE)
>
> lower_interval <- ate - t_multiplier*standard_error
> upper_interval <- ate + t_multiplier*standard_error
>
> cbind(lower_interval, upper_interval)
     lower_interval upper_interval
[ 1,]        3.44184       12.60598
```

d. Subtracting the baseline difference score from the posttest difference score, the difference-in-differences ATE estimate is 5.51 (compared to 8.02 previously) and the estimated standard error has decreased from 2.32 to 1.33, suggesting a lower treatment effect than that calculated in 4.1(c) but having better precision. The new 95% confidence interval ranges from 2.88 to 8.15.

```
> mean_treatment <- mean(murrar$diff_in_diff[ murrar$cond == 1], na.rm = TRUE)
> mean_control <- mean(murrar$diff_in_diff[ murrar$cond == 0], na.rm = TRUE)
>
> ate <- mean_treatment - mean_control
> ate
[ 1]  5.513232

> sd_treatment <- sd(murrar$diff_in_diff[ murrar$cond == 1], na.rm = TRUE)
> sd_control <- sd(murrar$diff_in_diff[ murrar$cond == 0], na.rm = TRUE)
>
> n_treatment <- nrow(murrar[ murrar$cond == 1 & !is.na(murrar$diff_in_diff), ])
> n_control <- nrow(murrar[ murrar$cond == 0 & !is.na(murrar$diff_in_diff), ])
>
> standard_error <- sqrt(sd_control^2/n_control + sd_treatment^2/n_treatment)
> standard_error
[ 1]  1.334663

> t_multiplier <- qt(0.025, (n_treatment + n_control - 2), lower.tail = FALSE)
>
> lower_interval <- ate - t_multiplier*standard_error
> upper_interval <- ate + t_multiplier*standard_error
>
> cbind(lower_interval, upper_interval)
     lower_interval upper_interval
[ 1,]        2.878696       8.147768
```

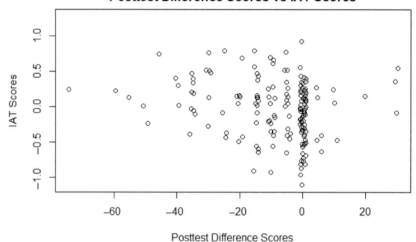

FIGURE S.5. Assessing the correlation between IAT scores and thermometer change scores

e. The thermometer rating uses explicit survey questions to gauge participants' attitudes toward Arab people. The IAT seeks to measure implicit attitudes – automatically activated positive or negative evaluations – using reaction times. However, the explicit measures focus on Arabs, whereas the implicit measures focus on Arab Muslims, which are a subset of Arabs. The plot in Figure S.5 indicates that higher IAT scores are associated with lower posttest difference scores, but the correlation is weak. Those with the highest posttest difference scores have average IAT scores that are slightly lower than those with the lowest posttest difference scores. A negative correlation makes sense here because reaction times lengthen with negative attitudes. It is not clear whether the weak correlation reflects the flaws in one or both measures or the fact that the two measures assess different attitudes/ feelings toward somewhat different groups.

```
> plot(x = jitter(murrar$diff_t1), y = murrar$iatT1N,
+      main = "Posttest Difference Scores vs IAT Scores",
+      xlab = "Posttest Difference Scores", ylab = "IAT Scores")
```

4.2 a. The difference between the mean FTar_1 and mean FTar score is 0.72, indicating a slight positive drift in attitudes over the two surveys.

```
mean(bruneau$FTar_1) - mean(bruneau$FTar)
[1] 0.7186992
```

b. Interspersing filler questions reduces the risk that participants will figure out the purpose of the study and give answers that do not reflect their actual views. The repetition of a few questions allows the researchers some comparable repeated responses, enabling them to gauge how responses changed from one interview to the next. At the same time, by changing the remaining questions in the subsequent interview, the researcher injects novelty into the survey that encourages the participants to freshly consider their responses to survey questions rather than falling back on their previous responses. (As pointed out in Chapter 7, any of the baseline measures, whether repeated or not, may serve as covariates when regression is used to estimate the ATE.)

c. Using a single essay by a confederate has the advantage of providing a consistent treatment whose effects are easily interpreted. Disadvantages include the use of deception – subjects who participate in future studies may become suspicious about the genuineness of the materials that they read. Treatment consistency also limits the generalizability of the results, as the treatment effect only captures the effects of one essay.

d. For White participants, the average treatment effect is estimated to be 7.87 (with a standard error of 4.09). The 95% confidence interval is between –0.37 and 16.11.

```
> white <- subset(bruneau, group == 1)
>
> ate <- mean(white$Average_1[ white$condition == 2] ) - mean(white$Average_1
[ white$condition == 1] )
> ate
[ 1] 7.868841

> sd_treatment <- sd(white$Average_1[ white$condition == 2] )
> sd_control <- sd(white$Average_1[ white$condition == 1] )
>
> n_treatment <- nrow(white[ white$condition == 2 & !is.na(white$Average_1), ] )
> n_control <- nrow(white[ white$condition == 1 & !is.na(white$Average_1), ] )
>
> standard_error <- sqrt(sd_control^2/n_control + sd_treatment^2/n_treatment)
> standard_error
[ 1] 4.090657

> t_multiplier <- qt(0.025, (n_treatment + n_control - 2), lower.tail = FALSE)
>
> lower_interval <- ate - t_multiplier*standard_error
> upper_interval <- ate + t_multiplier*standard_error
>
> cbind(lower_interval, upper_interval)
     lower_interval upper_interval
[ 1,]    -0.3701662     16.10785
```

For Mexican participants, the average treatment effect is estimated to be 4.43 (with a standard error of 2.05). The 95% confidence interval is between 0.35 and 8.52. The ATE appears to be positive for both the White and Mexican participants. The estimated ATE is greater among the White participants, although the larger standard error indicates that the estimate is less precise.

```
> mexican <- subset(bruneau, group == 2)
>
> ate <- mean(mexican$Average_1[ mexican$condition == 2] , na.rm = TRUE) -
mean(mexican$Average_1[ mexican$condition == 1] , na.rm = TRUE)
> ate
[ 1] 4.433501
>
> sd_treatment <- sd(mexican$Average_1[ mexican$condition == 2] , na.rm = TRUE)
```

```
> sd_control <- sd(mexican$Average_1[ mexican$condition == 1], na.rm = TRUE)
>
> n_treatment <- nrow(mexican[ mexican$condition == 2 & !is.na(mexican$Average_1),])
> n_control <- nrow(mexican[ mexican$condition == 1 & !is.na(mexican$Average_1),])
>
> standard_error <- sqrt(sd_control^2/n_control + sd_treatment^2/n_treatment)
> standard_error
[1] 2.049233
>
> t_multiplier <- qt(0.025, (n_treatment + n_control - 2), lower.tail = FALSE)
>
> lower_interval <- ate - t_multiplier*standard_error
> upper_interval <- ate + t_multiplier*standard_error
>
> cbind(lower_interval, upper_interval)
      lower_interval upper_interval
[1,]       0.3493856       8.517616
```

4.3 a. Among Republicans, the Liberal Trump condition appeared to increase support for background checks by 0.77 − 0.70 = 0.07, or 7 percentage points. The Conservative Trump condition changed support for background checks by 0.35 − 0.70 = −0.35, or a 35 percentage point decrease. For participants in the GOP Leaders Oppose condition, support for background checks changed by 0.60 − 0.70 = −0.10, or a 10 percentage point decrease. The greatest effect is seen among Republicans who received the Conservative Trump condition, where support decreased substantially from the control condition.

```
> rep <- subset(barber, republican == 1). # create a data frame with Republicans
> n_rep <- table(rep$condition)            # calculate the N within each condition
> t_rep <- table(rep$Support, rep$condition, useNA = "ifany") # table of Support by
    condition
> t_rep <- prop.table(t_rep, 2) # t_rep is input to create table of proportions, % by column
> colnames(t_rep) <- c("Liberal Trump", "Conservative Trump", "GOP Leaders",
"Control")
> rbind(t_rep, n_rep). # row-bind the table of proportions and the column totals
       Liberal Trump Conservative Trump  GOP Leaders     Control
0         0.18918919          0.5161290   0.34126984   0.22777778
1         0.77027027          0.3548387   0.60317460   0.70000000
<NA>      0.04054054          0.1290323   0.05555556   0.07222222
n_rep    74.00000000         62.0000000 126.00000000 180.00000000
```

b. Among non-Republicans, the estimated ATE of the Liberal Trump condition is 0.83 − 0.84 = −0.01. The Conservative Trump condition appears to have an ATE of 0.81 − 0.84 = −0.03, also a small decrease. As expected, the effects of Trump treatments are larger among Republicans than non-Republicans. GOP Leaders Oppose condition seems to produce a small effect as well: an estimate of 0.80 − 0.84 = −0.04, or a 4 percentage point decrease.

```
> nonrep <- subset(barber, republican == 0)
> n_nonrep <- table(nonrep$condition)
> t_nonrep <- table(nonrep$Support, nonrep$condition, useNA = "ifany")
> t_nonrep <- prop.table(t_nonrep, 2)
> colnames(t_nonrep) <- c("Liberal Trump", "Conservative Trump", "GOP Leaders", "Control")
>
> rbind(t_nonrep, n_nonrep)
```

	Liberal Trump	Conservative Trump	GOP Leaders	Control
0	0.08730159	0.12318841	0.10948905	0.078125
1	0.83333333	0.81159420	0.79562044	0.840625
<NA>	0.07936508	0.06521739	0.09489051	0.081250
n_nonrep	126.00000000	138.00000000	274.00000000	320.000000

c. Among Republican respondents, Trump's conservative stance appears to be far more influential than congressional leaders' conservative stance, decreasing support for background checks by 35 percentage points compared to 10 percentage points.

4.4 a. If skipping the video prevented subjects from absorbing its content, the video treatment effects would have been stronger if the researchers had not allowed respondents to skip the video.

b. ATE of `LText`:

```
> mean(mullinix$Q30[ mullinix$FL_10_DO == "LText"], na.rm = TRUE) -
mean(mullinix$Q30[ mullinix$FL_10_DO == "Control"], na.rm = TRUE)
[1] -0.7283672
```

ATE of `LVideo`:

```
> mean(mullinix$Q30[ mullinix$FL_10_DO == "LVideo"], na.rm = TRUE) -
mean(mullinix$Q30[ mullinix$FL_10_DO == "Control"], na.rm = TRUE)
[1] -0.6810916
```

ATE of `LTextVideo`:

```
> mean(mullinix$Q30[ mullinix$FL_10_DO == "LTextVideo"], na.rm = TRUE) -
mean(mullinix$Q30[ mullinix$FL_10_DO == "Control"], na.rm = TRUE)
[1] -0.800831
```

Mullinix et al.'s (2021) results suggest that the effects are not additive. While the ATE of `LTextVideo` shows slightly greater disapproval in the Text_and_Video group compared to either the Text or Video treatment alone, the estimated ATE for the Text_and_Video group (–0.80) is smaller than the estimated Video ATE plus the estimated Text ATE (–0.73 + (–0.68) = –1.41).

4.5 a. The treatment and control groups' background attributes have similar means and standard deviations.

```
> # rather than calculate the means and standard deviations for each variable one
at a time,
> # use the apply() function to show all 12 comparisons at once
> treatment_mean <- apply(balcells[ balcells$treatmentgroup == 1, 1:12], 2, mean,
na.rm = TRUE)
> treatment_sd <- apply(balcells[ balcells$treatmentgroup == 1, 1:12], 2, sd, na.rm
= TRUE)
> control_mean <- apply(balcells[ balcells$treatmentgroup == 0, 1:12], 2, mean, na.
rm = TRUE)
> control_sd <- apply(balcells[ balcells$treatmentgroup == 0, 1:12], 2, sd, na.rm =
TRUE)
>
> cbind(treatment_mean, treatment_sd, control_mean, control_sd)
                     treatment_mean treatment_sd control_mean control_sd
age                       20.8982999    1.9380423   21.0872100  3.4153089
```

```
gender                      1.6304348    0.4844455    1.6428571   0.4974219
pre_ideology_1              5.0652174    1.9897787    4.5222705   2.0224365
pre_economic_situation      2.3851852    0.8462841    2.4800000   0.8481479
pre_political_interest      1.4029851    0.7669822    1.4960000   0.7253920
pre_religion_importance     1.6000000    1.0452451    1.4959350   1.0352317
totalmuseums                4.9923664    2.3254319    5.3333333   2.3669053
pre_conf_gov                0.9548872    0.7163106    0.9440000   0.6756598
pre_inst_gov                0.1417910    0.3501447    0.1370968   0.3453448
pre_current_ineq            3.5259259    0.8879763    3.7096774   0.5811986
pre_positive               18.5652174    7.6844297   19.5158730   7.4873057
pre_negative                6.7536232    5.4004752    6.9523810   5.7672970
```

b. Restricting our attention to the subjects who responded to the final survey, we see that the treatment and control groups' background attributes have similar means and standard deviations.

```
> survey3 <- subset(balcells, f3 == 1)
>
> treatment_mean <- apply(survey3[ survey3$treatmentgroup == 1, 1:12], 2, mean, na.rm =
TRUE)
> treatment_sd <- apply(survey3[ survey3$treatmentgroup == 1, 1:12], 2, sd, na.rm =
TRUE)
> control_mean <- apply(survey3[ survey3$treatmentgroup == 0, 1:12], 2, mean, na.rm
= TRUE)
> control_sd <- apply(survey3[ survey3$treatmentgroup == 0, 1:12], 2, sd, na.rm =
TRUE)
>
> cbind(treatment_mean, treatment_sd, control_mean, control_sd)
                        treatment_mean treatment_sd control_mean control_sd
age                        20.9998352    1.9708018   21.6883354   4.5297130
gender                      1.6714286    0.4730851    1.7213115   0.4875499
pre_ideology_1              5.1857143    1.8904248    4.2786885   2.1065861
pre_economic_situation      2.4000000    0.8235659    2.4426230   0.8855241
pre_political_interest      1.3478261    0.7441159    1.5737705   0.7628678
pre_religion_importance     1.7142857    1.0651646    1.4754098   1.1196213
totalmuseums                5.2352941    2.5163207    5.2711864   2.2805815
pre_conf_gov                1.0000000    0.7019641    1.0491803   0.6171502
pre_inst_gov                0.1714286    0.3796042    0.1333333   0.3428033
pre_current_ineq            3.6000000    0.8747670    3.7833333   0.4544196
pre_positive               19.2571429    6.8285117   19.5573770   7.7082739
pre_negative                6.7142857    5.1362391    6.4262295   5.1168318
```

4.6 a. If the police raid treatment also causes local residents to become hesitant to report crime, the crime rate on treated blocks would be underestimated, which would exaggerate the deterrent effect of police raids. If the raids truly had no effect on crime, reduced reporting in the treatment group would suggest that raids were effective in preventing crime.

b. The average weekly number of crimes on treatment blocks is 3.10 and on control blocks is 2.83. The average treatment effect of raids on weekly crimes per block is therefore estimated to be 0.27. The standard error is 0.49. The 95% confidence interval is between –0.70 and 1.23, which includes zero.

```
> mean_treatment <- mean(sherman$CFS_after_5weeks[ sherman$treatment == 1] )
> mean_treatment
[ 1]  3.098077
>
> mean_control <- mean(sherman$CFS_after_5weeks[ sherman$treatment == 0] )
> mean_control
```

```
[1]  2.831068
>
> ate <- mean_treatment - mean_control
> ate
[1]  0.267009
>
> sd_treatment <- sd(sherman$CFS_after_5weeks[ sherman$treatment == 1])
> sd_control <- sd(sherman$CFS_after_5weeks[ sherman$treatment == 0])
>
> n_treatment <- length(sherman$treatment[ sherman$treatment == 1])
> n_control <- length(sherman$treatment[ sherman$treatment == 0])
>
> standard_error <- sqrt(sd_control^2/n_control + sd_treatment^2/n_treatment)
> standard_error
[1]  0.4907575
>
> t_multiplier <- qt(0.025, (n_treatment + n_control - 2), lower.tail = FALSE)
>
> lower_interval <- ate - t_multiplier*standard_error
> upper_interval <- ate + t_multiplier*standard_error
>
> cbind(lower_interval, upper_interval)
     lower_interval upper_interval
[1,]     -0.7005702       1.234588
```

c. Observing only outcomes of the treatment condition over 10 weeks, we might be led to infer that the treatment reduces crime slightly, especially in the two weeks immediately following the raid. Five weeks prior to the week of the raid had an average of $(2.923077 + 2.759615 + 3.250000 + 2.855769 + 3.346154)/5 = 3.03$ crimes reported, and the four weeks following the raid had an average of $(2.798077 + 2.865385 + 3.086538 + 3.201923)/4 = 2.99$ crimes reported.

d. However, the control group's crime rates over time cast doubt on the idea that the treatment had a deterrent effect. A similar pattern of over time drift appears to hold for the control condition. Decreased crime reporting can also be seen two weeks after the non-raid week. The five weeks prior to the non-raid week had an average of $(2.679612 + 2.737864 + 2.679612 + 3.058252 + 2.941748)/5 = 2.82$ crimes reported, and the four weeks following had an average of $(2.621359 + 2.475728 + 2.970874 + 2.970874)/4 = 2.76$.

Over-time comparisons on their own can be misleading. The beauty of this study is that the randomly assigned control group indicates what would have happened in the treatment group had the treatment not been administered. The fact that we see similar trajectories in both treatment and control crime rates suggests that the raids failed to deter crime.

4.7 a. The average hectare forest loss in treated areas is 1,274,296, and the loss in control areas is 1,507,191. The average treatment effect is therefore estimated to be −232,895, with a standard error of 384,831. The 95% confidence interval is −996,389 to 530,598.

```
> mean_treatment <- mean(wrenlewis$tcl_area_L_from2010to2017[ wrenlewis$treated == 1])
> mean_treatment
[1]  1274296
>
> mean_control <- mean(wrenlewis$tcl_area_L_from2010to2017[ wrenlewis$treated == 0])
> mean_control
```

```
[1]  1507191
>
> ate <- mean_treatment - mean_control
> ate
[1]  -232895.1
>
> sd_treatment <- sd(wrenlewis$tcl_area_L_from2010to2017[ wrenlewis$treated == 1] )
> sd_control <- sd(wrenlewis$tcl_area_L_from2010to2017[ wrenlewis$treated == 0] )
>
> n_treatment <- length(wrenlewis$treated[ wrenlewis$treated == 1] )
> n_control <- length(wrenlewis$treated[ wrenlewis$treated == 0] )
>
> standard_error <- sqrt(sd_control^2/n_control + sd_treatment^2/n_treatment)
> standard_error
[1]  384830.9
>
> t_multiplier <- qt(0.025, (n_treatment + n_control - 2), lower.tail = FALSE)
>
> lower_interval <- ate - t_multiplier*standard_error
> upper_interval <- ate + t_multiplier*standard_error
>
> cbind(lower_interval, upper_interval)
     lower_interval upper_interval
[1,]      -996388.5       530598.4
```

b. Using change scores, the average hectare forest loss in treated areas is estimated to be $-381,029$, and the loss in control areas is $-19,998$. The average treatment effect is therefore estimated to be $-361,031$. Its standard error is $285,839$, and the 95% confidence interval is $-928,127$ to $206,065$.

The use of change scores decreases the variance in outcomes and leads to a more precise estimate of the ATE.

```
> wrenlewis$change_score <- wrenlewis$tcl_area_L_from2010to2017 -
wrenlewis$tcl_area_L_from2001to2009
>
> mean_treatment <- mean(wrenlewis$change_score[ wrenlewis$treated == 1] )
> mean_treatment
[1]  -381029.3
>
> mean_control <- mean(wrenlewis$change_score[ wrenlewis$treated == 0] )
> mean_control
[1]  -19998.33
>
> ate <- mean_treatment - mean_control
> ate
[1]  -361031
>
> sd_treatment <- sd(wrenlewis$change_score[ wrenlewis$treated == 1] )
> sd_control <- sd(wrenlewis$change_score[ wrenlewis$treated == 0] )
>
> n_treatment <- length(wrenlewis$treated[ wrenlewis$treated == 1] )
> n_control <- length(wrenlewis$treated[ wrenlewis$treated == 0] )
>
> standard_error <- sqrt(sd_control^2/n_control + sd_treatment^2/n_treatment)
> standard_error
[1]  285839
>
> t_multiplier <- qt(0.025, (n_treatment + n_control - 2), lower.tail = FALSE)
>
> lower_interval <- ate - t_multiplier*standard_error
```

```
> upper_interval <- ate + t_multiplier*standard_error
>
> cbind(lower_interval, upper_interval)
     lower_interval upper_interval
[1,]      -928127.4      206065.5
```

CHAPTER 5

5.1 Poori cooking in Chapter 3 does not qualify as an experiment involving human subjects. The subjects in this study are the balls of poori dough; these subjects are randomly assigned to different cooking temperatures. Human involvement was limited to a research assistant who rated all of the pooris. From this standpoint, the dough balls revealed their potential outcomes, and the research assistant simply measured these outcomes.

5.2 The *Little Mosque on the Prairie* study does not qualify for review as a "benign intervention," which are usually brief, harmless interventions that do not have lasting effects. First, the experiment is lengthy, insofar as it requires participants to watch six episodes of a sitcom. The study also anticipates that exposure to the lives of an outgroup will change their perceptions of (and perhaps longer-term attitudes toward) Arabs. Finally, the experiment used deception to mask the true research question being studied. The fact that the study does not qualify as a benign intervention does not imply that there are serious ethical problems with the study, but it does mean that that the study does not qualify for expedited approval under the benign intervention standard.

5.3 Minimal risk "means that the probability and magnitude of harm or discomfort anticipated in the research are not greater in and of themselves than those ordinarily encountered in daily life or during the performance of routine physical or psychological examinations or tests." The criteria are therefore the magnitude of harm and the probability that harm will occur.

5.4 Yes, in the short run, the extraction of a control group means fewer subjects will be exposed to a potentially harmful message. But, in the long run, this line of research might lead to the discovery of more effective ways of advertising cigarettes, which may mean more harm to future subjects as well as nonsubjects (potential cigarette consumers).

5.5 Confidential information is private information about subjects that is collected in the course of research, usually through some kind of personal communication. This information may be known to researchers involved in the study but must not be disclosed to others without a subject's consent. Anonymity means that information that could be used to identify subjects (such as photos) is not disclosed publicly.

5.6 Children are considered a vulnerable population as they may be unable to weigh the costs and benefits of participation in a study and are legally unable to give informed consent. Extra care must be taken when undertaking studies that include underage participants, including getting parental consent and avoiding potentially harmful interventions.

5.7 A waiver for documentation of informed consent may be granted if "the research could not practicably be carried out without the waiver or alteration." For example, some studies present minimal risk and do not collect identifiable information; collecting informed consent documentation under these circumstances may be impractical. Also, in studies where the primary risk of harm is the breach of confidentiality and the consent form is the only record that links the participant's identity to the sensitive information, a waiver may be granted.

5.8 A researcher debriefs the participant after an experiment to explain the purpose of the study and to clear up any false or misleading impressions that might have been created by the intervention or the instructions. When experiments involve deception, debriefing is usually required.

5.9 In Murrar and Brauer's (2018) experiment on the effect of *Little Mosque* on attitudes toward Arabs, the researchers used deception in their instructions to the participants. They characterized their study as an attempt to "examine television-watching behaviors" so as to distract the participants from the real aims of the experiment (changing attitudes about Arab Muslims). The researchers also created the impression that many sitcoms were being evaluated, again to downplay the fact that *Little Mosque* and its effects on social attitudes were the focus of the study. The first form of deception seems necessary in order to prevent participants from giving insincere survey responses. The second form of deception could have been avoided had a wider assortment of placebo shows been included; rather than show *Friends* to half of the participants, the researchers could have shown a few different sitcoms featuring White characters.

5.10 Conflict of interest arises when researchers have, themselves or through close family, financial stakes that could bias their scientific judgment. A researcher might stand to gain from an investment related to the research project (e.g., a researcher owns shares in the firm supplying materials for the study) or the researcher's investment might be affected by the results of the research (e.g., a researcher is also a director of a business whose product is evaluated by the research).

5.11 The file drawer problem refers to a form of publication bias, whereby research findings that are deemed unpublishable go unreported (i.e., they remain in the file drawer). This problem is thought to be especially common when studies show weak average treatment effects, because scientific publications tend to be reluctant to publish "null" findings, thereby reducing the incentives for authors to submit papers reporting null findings. The resulting literature therefore exaggerates the effectiveness of treatments because estimates showing positive effects are more likely to be published.

5.12   a. One ethical concern is the lack of informed consent from the participants. The individuals at hiring firms are not informed about their participation in a study, nor are they debriefed about the deceptive intervention to which they have been exposed.

        b. In addition to the concern in point (a), experiments that study the response rates of public officials to fictitious constituents can have wider implications for non-participants. Officials with limited resources may allocate time to respond to fictitious correspondence rather than real concerns from their constituents. If public officials begin to suspect that the correspondence they receive comes from researchers rather than real constituents, they might allocate less time to responding to correspondence, which may adversely affect constituents.

CHAPTER 6

6.1 The described study does not obtain consent from YouTube users who become experimental participants. These participants are exposed to a deceptive intervention that may affect bystanders, such as the individual who uploaded the video, by arbitrarily diminishing their video's rating. Due to the nature of the platform, it is unlikely that the researcher can feasibly obtain consent. An adjustment could be to conduct the experiment in a lab setting or through an online survey where all participants are aware that they are participating in research and can provide consent. Another adjustment would be to invite people to watch posted videos and give their honest feedback, then randomly encourage some of them to post their evaluations to YouTube. This adjustment does not overcome all consent-related concerns but does overcome concerns stemming from the use of deception.

6.2 The design of three-day messaging periods seems to violate the random assignment assumption. The days assigned to each experimental condition seem to be assigned according to a pre-specified order, not according to a random sequence. Assuming the center is open Monday to Friday, the three-day period may cover different days of the week and include participants of different backgrounds. For example, the control condition may be on Monday–Wednesday and the promotional brochure Thursday–Monday. If certain groups of individuals are more likely to visit the center on Friday, they will not be represented in the control condition. As a result, there may be a systematic relationship between subjects' potential outcomes and the intervention to which they are exposed.

6.3 There are advantages and disadvantages to each approach. Counting towels has the advantage of being noninvasive and inexpensive compared to stationing an observer. An observer may more accurately measure which machines have been cleaned, but the presence of an observer may prompt the patrons to behave differently if they are aware of being watched. Using video footage may provide accurate measurements but raises concerns about protecting the anonymity of subjects. None of the approaches addresses concerns about informed consent, but the latter two approaches are weakest in this regard since they measure individual behavior.

6.4 Further conversation could jeopardize symmetry if the waitstaff behaved differently toward customers who got the smiley face compared to those who did not. The average treatment effect would reflect not only the influence of the smiley face on the bill but also any differences in subsequent waitstaff behavior.

6.5 The dining halls do not seem to have been randomly assigned to the intervention, which violates the random assignment assumption. The lack of random assignment may lead to biased estimates if students at one dining hall are systematically different from those at the other dining hall.

6.6 a. The decision to exclude noncontributors in calculating the average can lead to biased inferences if the treatment affects the proportion of contributors. The researchers have introduced a form of attrition by deleting the outcomes of noncontributors, which jeopardizes the random assignment assumption.

b. The average donation amount among all participants in the experiment in the challenge (treattype 1) and matching (treattype 2) conditions supports the researchers' conclusion that the challenge condition performs best. Challenge also outperforms the low control (treattype 3) and high control (treattype 0) conditions.

```
> mean(rondeau$donation[ rondeau$treattype == 0], na.rm = TRUE)
[1]  1.838235
> mean(rondeau$donation[ rondeau$treattype == 1], na.rm = TRUE)
[1]  2.162884
> mean(rondeau$donation[ rondeau$treattype == 2], na.rm = TRUE)
[1]  1.646667
> mean(rondeau$donation[ rondeau$treattype == 3], na.rm = TRUE)
[1]  1.26506
```

c. The 95% confidence interval of using a challenge appeal versus a matching gift appeal ranges from −0.60 to 1.64. As this confidence interval brackets 0, it is possible that there is no true difference between the effects of the challenge appeal and the matching appeal.

```
> t.test(rondeau$donation[ rondeau$treattype == 1], rondeau$donation
   [ rondeau$treattype == 2])

Welch Two Sample t-test

data:  rondeau$donation[ rondeau$treattype == 1] and rondeau$donation
   [ rondeau$treattype == 2]
t = 0.90461, df = 1285.2, p-value = 0.3658
alternative hypothesis: true difference in means is not equal to 0
95 percent confidence interval:
-0.6032943  1.6357286
```

6.7 a. Average total sales on treatment days was 612.00.

```
> mean(mcgrath$grandtotal[ mcgrath$treatment == 1])
[1]  612.0019
```

b. Standard deviation of total sales on treatment days was 152.13.

```
> sd(mcgrath$grandtotal[ mcgrath$treatment == 1])
[1]  152.1347
```

c. Average total sales on control days was 575.39.

```
> mean(mcgrath$grandtotal[ mcgrath$treatment == 0])
[1]  575.3879
```

d. Standard deviation of total sales on control days was 130.27.

```
> sd(mcgrath$grandtotal[ mcgrath$treatment == 0])
[1]  130.2705
```

e. The estimated ATE is 36.61; its standard error is 51.56; and the 95% confidence interval ranges from –69.01 to 142.24.

```
> ate <- mean_treatment - mean_control
> ate
[1]  36.61402
>
> n_treatment <- length(mcgrath$treatment[ mcgrath$treatment == 1])
> n_control <- length(mcgrath$treatment[ mcgrath$treatment == 0])
>
> standard_error <- sqrt(sd_control^2/n_control + sd_treatment^2/n_treatment)
> standard_error
[1]  51.5629
>
> t_multiplier <- qt(0.025, (n_treatment + n_control - 2), lower.tail = FALSE)
>
> lower_interval <- ate - t_multiplier*standard_error
> upper_interval <- ate + t_multiplier*standard_error
>
> cbind(lower_interval, upper_interval)
     lower_interval upper_interval
[1,]      -69.00779      142.2358
```

6.8 a. For food, the ATE is 21.76; its standard error is 17.56; the 95% confidence interval ranges from –14.21 to 57.72.

```
> ate <- mean(mcgrath$food[ mcgrath$treatment == 1]) - mean(mcgrath$food
[ mcgrath$treatment == 0])
> ate
[1]  21.75554
>
> sd_treatment <- sd(mcgrath$food[ mcgrath$treatment == 1])
> sd_control <- sd(mcgrath$food[ mcgrath$treatment == 0])
>
> standard_error <- sqrt(sd_control^2/n_control + sd_treatment^2/n_treatment)
> standard_error
[1]  17.55776
>
> t_multiplier <- qt(0.025, (n_treatment + n_control - 2), lower.tail = FALSE)
>
> lower_interval <- ate - t_multiplier*standard_error
> upper_interval <- ate + t_multiplier*standard_error
>
> cbind(lower_interval, upper_interval)
     lower_interval upper_interval
[1,]      -14.20991      57.72099
```

For books, the ATE is 20.37; its standard error is 32.01; the 95% confidence interval ranges from –45.19 to 85.93.

```
> ate <- mean(mcgrath$book[ mcgrath$treatment == 1]) - mean(mcgrath$book
[ mcgrath$treatment == 0])
> ate
[1]  20.36866
>
> sd_treatment <- sd(mcgrath$book[ mcgrath$treatment == 1])
```

```
> sd_control <- sd(mcgrath$book[ mcgrath$treatment == 0])
>
> standard_error <- sqrt(sd_control^2/n_control + sd_treatment^2/n_treatment)
> standard_error
[1] 32.00643
>
> t_multiplier <- qt(0.025, (n_treatment + n_control - 2), lower.tail = FALSE)
>
> lower_interval <- ate - t_multiplier*standard_error
> upper_interval <- ate + t_multiplier*standard_error
>
> cbind(lower_interval, upper_interval)
     lower_interval upper_interval
[1,]      -45.19354       85.93086
```

For coffee, the ATE is −5.51; its standard error is 21.13; the 95% confidence interval ranges from −48.80 to 37.78.

```
> ate <- mean(mcgrath$coffee[ mcgrath$treatment == 1]) - mean(mcgrath$coffee
[ mcgrath$treatment == 0])
> ate
[1] -5.510179
>
> sd_treatment <- sd(mcgrath$coffee[ mcgrath$treatment == 1])
> sd_control <- sd(mcgrath$coffee[ mcgrath$treatment == 0])
>
> standard_error <- sqrt(sd_control^2/n_control + sd_treatment^2/n_treatment)
> standard_error
[1] 21.1332
>
> t_multiplier <- qt(0.025, (n_treatment + n_control - 2), lower.tail = FALSE)
>
> lower_interval <- ate - t_multiplier*standard_error
> upper_interval <- ate + t_multiplier*standard_error
>
> cbind(lower_interval, upper_interval)
     lower_interval upper_interval
[1,]      -48.79957       37.77921
```

b. Both food and books appear to have similar sized ATEs at 21.76 and 20.37, respectively. After calculating the percentage increase over the average sales on control days, food is the most affected by the chocolate aroma, at a 30.2 percent increase, compared to 12.1 percent for books and −1.6 percent for coffee.

```
> ate_food/ mean(mcgrath$food[ mcgrath$treatment == 0])
[1] 0.3023672
>
> ate_book/ mean(mcgrath$book[ mcgrath$treatment == 0])
[1] 0.1207456
>
> ate_coffee/ mean(mcgrath$coffee[ mcgrath$treatment == 0])
[1] -0.0164607
```

c. Since all three of the confidence intervals include 0, we cannot rule out the possibility that the true ATE of the chocolate aroma treatment is zero (i.e., no effect on sales). Although an ATE of zero lies within our 95% confidence interval, our best guesses as to the ATE in each category of sales are still the estimates calculated in part (b).

6.9 a. The main hypothesis is that diffusion of chocolate aroma will increase overall sales.
   b. A Canadian bookstore-café.
   c. Chocolate aroma was diffused (from two sites) during days randomly assigned to treatment. No aromas were diffused on control days.
   d. Random assignment of days was conducted by a coin flip each day.
   e. The manipulation check involved a small survey of patrons, which verified that they either detected the aroma or noticed it after being prompted.
   f. Outcomes were overall sales each day. These sales were also subdivided according to whether they consisted of food, books, or dry goods.
   g. A substantial percentage increase in overall sales, but the authors downplay this finding on the grounds that the confidence interval is very wide and includes zero.
   h. There are no glaring threats to core assumptions. One might wonder whether aromas from treatment days linger on subsequent control days (a threat to interference). The fact that the staff were blind to the experiment helps preserve symmetry.
   i. The findings seem to replicate a previous study in Belgium, but neither study isolates the treatment effect with precision.
   j. Because the store owners collaborated on the study, they bore any risk of financial harm that could have come from a loss of sales. The patrons were not informed ahead of time or afterward, but stores routinely vary their promotions without acquiring consent, and the intervention was neither risky nor deceptive.

CHAPTER 7

7.1 Using the difference-in-means method, the estimated ATE is 6.366. Regression produces the same result when the T_i is scored 0 for control and 1 for treatment. However, when T_i has been rescored to −1 for control and 1 for treatment, the coefficient for cond_rescored is 3.183, which is half as large as the difference-in-means results. The coefficient is half as large because the estimate reflects the effect of moving two units (from −1 control to 1 treatment) rather than one unit (0 control to 1 treatment).

```
> murrar$Y <- murrar$arab_t1
> murrar$T <- murrar$condition
> summary(lm(Y ~ T, data = murrar))

Coefficients:
            Estimate Std. Error t value Pr(>|t|)
(Intercept)   64.157      2.139  29.990   <2e-16 ***
T              6.366      3.052   2.086   0.0384 *
---
Signif. codes:  0 '***' 0.001 '**' 0.01 '*' 0.05 '.' 0.1 ' ' 1

Residual standard error: 20.18 on 173 degrees of freedom
  (18 observations deleted due to missingness)
```

```
Multiple R-squared:  0.02454,     Adjusted R-squared:  0.0189
F-statistic: 4.352 on 1 and 173 DF,  p-value: 0.03844


> murrar$T_rescored <- ifelse(murrar$condition == 0, -1, 1)
> summary(lm(Y ~ T_rescored, data = murrar))


Coefficients:
            Estimate Std. Error t value Pr(>|t|)
(Intercept)   67.340      1.526  44.134   <2e-16 ***
T_rescored     3.183      1.526   2.086   0.0384 *
---
Signif. codes:  0 '***' 0.001 '**' 0.01 '*' 0.05 '.' 0.1 ' ' 1


Residual standard error: 20.18 on 173 degrees of freedom
  (18 observations deleted due to missingness)
Multiple R-squared:  0.02454,     Adjusted R-squared:  0.0189
F-statistic: 4.352 on 1 and 173 DF,  p-value: 0.03844
```

7.2 a. The estimated average treatment effect is 0.718 and estimated standard error is 0.252. In other words, crouching increased the average tip by \$0.72.

```
[summary(lm(formula = tip ~ crouch, data = lynn))


Coefficients:
            Estimate Std. Error t value        Pr(>|t|)
(Intercept)   2.5580     0.1720  14.873 < 0.0000000000000002 ***
crouch        0.7184     0.2519   2.852             0.00497 **
---
Signif. codes:  0 '***' 0.001 '**' 0.01 '*' 0.05 '.' 0.1 ' ' 1


Residual standard error: 1.529 on 146 degrees of freedom
Multiple R-squared:  0.05278,
Adjusted R-squared:  0.04629
F-statistic: 8.135 on 1 and 146 DF,  p-value: 0.004973
```

b. The number of customers and time of each shift are pre-treatment covariates. The amount of the bill, whether the bill was paid by credit card, and whether the bill was paid by a man or woman are post-treatment covariates, as these where choices made after the treatment was administered. The two pre-treatment covariates were determined prior to treatment and could not have been affected by treatment. However, the post-treatment covariates may be affected by the treatment. For example, waitstaff posture may influence the number of items that customers order, thus affecting the size of the bill. Alternatively, in a group of customers that includes both genders, the posture treatment may cause females in the group to choose to pay rather than males, or vice versa. Finally, it is possible that a choice to pay by cash or credit card is influenced by waitstaff posture. While it is possible that certain post-treatment covariates are unaffected by treatment, this is a matter of conjecture rather than something that follows from the experimental design.

c. The dataset contains no missing values. The estimated ATE of the regression model with covariate adjustment is 0.697, with a standard error of 0.185.

```
summary(lm(formula = tip ~ crouch + groupsize + daytime, data = lynn))
```

```
Coefficients:
            Estimate Std. Error t value      Pr(>|t|)
(Intercept) 0.010322   0.271315  0.038       0.969705
crouch      0.696732   0.185333  3.759        0.000247 ***
groupsize   0.957725   0.084910 11.279 < 0.0000000000000002 ***
daytime     0.003473   0.185343  0.019       0.985075
—
Signif. codes:  0 '***' 0.001 '**' 0.01 '*' 0.05 '.' 0.1 ' ' 1


Residual standard error: 1.121 on 144 degrees of freedom
Multiple R-squared:  0.4979,    Adjusted R-squared:  0.4874
F-statistic:  47.6 on 3 and 144 DF,  p-value: < 0.00000000000000022
```

d. Adjusting the ATE using covariates decreased the estimated ATE slightly, from 0.718 to 0.697. Covariate adjustment increased the precision of the estimate substantially; the estimated standard error decreased from 0.252 to 0.185. Comparing Figure S.6 to Figure S.7, we see that covariate adjustment reduces the vertical distance between the points and the fitted regression line.

```
> plot(x = jitter(lynn$crouch), y = lynn$tip,
+       abline(lm(tip ~ crouch, data = lynn)),
+       main = "Unadjusted ATE", xlab = "Crouch", ylab = "Tip")
> T_resid <- lynn$crouch - lm(crouch ~ groupsize + daytime, lynn)$fitted
> Y_resid <- lynn$tip - lm(tip ~ groupsize + daytime, lynn)$fitted
>
> resres <- lm(Y_resid ~ T_resid)
>
> plot(x = T_resid, y = Y_resid,
+       abline(resres),
+       main = "Adjusted ATE", xlab = "T Residuals", ylab = "Y Residuals")
```

e. The estimated ATE of 0.697 suggests that the waitstaff's position of crouching increases their tip by about $0.70. Compared to the average tip of $2.56 for customers in the control condition, this represents a change of 27 percent, a substantial increase.

f. The regression output calculated in (c) shows a p-value of 0.000247. If there were truly no effect of crouching, the chances of obtaining an estimate as large (in absolute value) as 0.697 simply due to a lucky random assignment is less than 1-in-1,000.

7.3 a. The coefficient b of −0.105 is the estimated marginal effect of Roomate_BMI. This coefficient can be interpreted as follows: Every 1 unit increase in Roomate_BMI on average generates a 0.105 decrease in Current_BMI.

```
> summary(lm(Current_BMI ~ Roommate_BMI, frijters))

Coefficients:
             Estimate Std. Error t value      Pr(>|t|)
(Intercept) 24.87988    2.14251  11.613 <0.0000000000000002 ***
Roommate_BMI -0.10529   0.09666  -1.089       0.277


—
Signif. codes:  0 '***' 0.001 '**' 0.01 '*' 0.05 '.' 0.1 ' ' 1
```

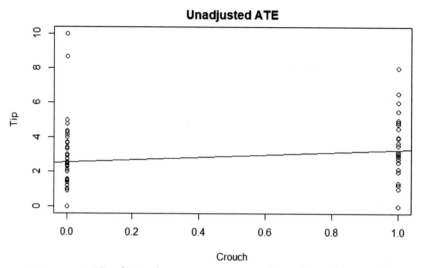

FIGURE S.6. Visualizing the average treatment effect of crouching on tips

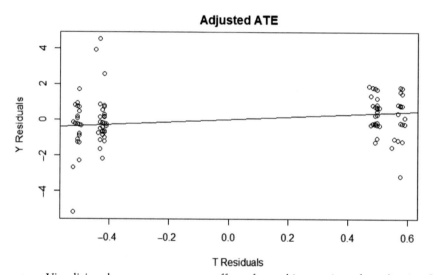

FIGURE S.7. Visualizing the average treatment effect of crouching on tips, after adjusting for covariates

```
Residual standard error: 4.069 on 212 degrees of freedom
Multiple R-squared:  0.005566,   Adjusted R-squared:  0.0008754
F-statistic: 1.187 on 1 and 212 DF,  p-value: 0.2772
```

b. When Roommate_BMI = 14.5:

Current_BMI = 24.87988 + (−0.10529) * 14.5 = 23.353175

When Roommate_BMI = 34.4:

Current_BMI = 24.87988 + (−0.10529) * 34.4 = 21.257904

c. When Past_BMI is added to the regression, the estimate of b changes from −0.105 to −0.130. The estimated standard error decreases from 0.097 to 0.057, indicating that the inclusion of this covariate improves the precision with which *b* is estimated.

```
> summary(lm(Current_BMI ~ Roommate_BMI + Past_BMI, data = frijters))

Coefficients:
             Estimate Std. Error t value           Pr(>|t|)
(Intercept)   8.47439    1.49305   5.676     0.0000000452 ***
Roommate_BMI -0.12952    0.05655  -2.290            0.023 *
Past_BMI      0.77369    0.03827  20.215 < 0.0000000000000002 ***
—
Signif. codes:  0 '***' 0.001 '**' 0.01 '*' 0.05 '.' 0.1 ' ' 1

Residual standard error: 2.38 on 211 degrees of freedom
Multiple R-squared:  0.6614,     Adjusted R-squared:  0.6582
F-statistic:   206 on 2 and 211 DF,  p-value: < 0.00000000000000022
```

7.4 a. For the `LVideo` condition, the estimated ATE is –0.681.

```
> mean(mullinix$Q30[ mullinix$FL_10_DO == "LVideo"], na.rm = TRUE) -
mean(mullinix$Q30[ mullinix$FL_10_DO == "Control"], na.rm = TRUE)
[1] -0.6810916
```

For the `LText` condition, the estimated ATE is –0.723.
```
> mean(mullinix$Q30[ mullinix$FL_10_DO == "LText"], na.rm = TRUE) -
mean(mullinix$Q30[ mullinix$FL_10_DO == "Control"], na.rm = TRUE)
[1] -0.7283672
```

For the `LTextVideo` condition, the estimated ATE is –0.801.

```
> mean(mullinix$Q30[ mullinix$FL_10_DO == "LTextVideo"], na.rm = TRUE) -
mean(mullinix$Q30[ mullinix$FL_10_DO == "Control"], na.rm = TRUE)
[1] -0.800831
```

b. The coefficients from the regression output are the same as the difference-in-means estimates.

```
> mullinix_l <- subset(mullinix, FL_10_DO %in% c("LVideo", "LText", "LTextVideo",
    "Control"))
>
> mullinix_l$LVideo <- ifelse(mullinix_l$FL_10_DO == "LVideo", 1, 0)
> mullinix_l$LText <- ifelse(mullinix_l$FL_10_DO == "LText", 1, 0)
> mullinix_l$LTextVideo <- ifelse(mullinix_l$FL_10_DO == "LTextVideo", 1, 0)
>
> summary(lm(Q30 ~ LVideo + LText + LTextVideo, data = mullinix_l))

Call:
lm(formula = Q30 ~ LVideo + LText + LTextVideo, data = mullinix_l)

Residuals:
    Min      1Q  Median      3Q     Max
-3.3950 -1.6667  0.2861  1.4058  3.4058

Coefficients:
             Estimate Std. Error t value           Pr(>|t|)
(Intercept)   4.39503    0.08976  48.966 < 0.0000000000000002 ***
LVideo       -0.68109    0.12898  -5.281     0.000000145295 ***
LText        -0.72837    0.12797  -5.692     0.000000014774 ***
```

```
LTextVideo  -0.80083    0.12914  -6.201       0.000000000702 ***

  _

Signif. codes:  0 '***' 0.001 '**' 0.01 '*' 0.05 '.' 0.1 ' ' 1

Residual standard error: 1.889 on 1698 degrees of freedom
  (77 observations deleted due to missingness)
Multiple R-squared:  0.02897,   Adjusted R-squared:  0.02726
F-statistic: 16.89 on 3 and 1698 DF,  p-value: 0.00000000008246
```

7.5 a. All else being equal, an increase in the sum of squared residuals increases the numerator of the equation and will cause an increase in the standard error.

   b. All else being equal, an increase in k increases the numerator of the equation and will cause an increase in the standard error.

   c. With all other equation components held equal, the reduction in the standard deviation of T_{resid} compared to that of T_i causes the standard error to increase.

   d. Using blocked randomization so that the standard deviation of T_{resid} = standard deviation of T_i = 0.2513629 after covariate adjustment, the standard error would be 1.602.

$$\text{standard error} = \sqrt{\frac{19185.2324/(175-4)}{(174)(0.2513629)}} = 1.601622878$$

7.6   a. As the 150 disclosed participants were randomly selected from the 300 participants, we would expect that they are the same as the 150 undisclosed participants. Since their apparent ATE is 5, with a standard error of 4, we would expect the undisclosed participant's ATE to also be 5 with the same standard error. Therefore, we expect that a positive estimate is more likely than a negative estimate.

   b. If the first 150 observations had produced an estimated ATE of 0 with a standard error of 4, we would infer that the unobserved observations had an ATE of 0 and, thus, are equally likely to generate a positive or negative estimate.

7.7 a. The effects of exposure to *Little Mosque* on participants' ratings of warmth toward Arabs are large enough to be substantively meaningful but not large enough to be called "tranformative." The regression based on Eq. (7.4) generates an estimated ATE of 5.72. Comparing this estimate to the standard deviation of the control group, we find that the apparent treatment effect is equal to 26 percent of the control group's standard deviation.

```
> sd(murrar$arab_t1[ murrar$condition==0] ,na.rm=TRUE)
[ 1]  21.64061
> 5.71666/21.64061
[ 1]  0.2641635
```

   b. The broadcast of *Little Mosque* to a large audience increases the importance of the treatment effect found by the experiment. If the treatment effects are generalizable, then the changes in warmth toward Arabs after watching this sitcom may extend to large numbers of Canadians.

c. The next ATE estimate focuses on evaluations of Arabs after four to six weeks. Using Eq. (7.4) but replacing `arab_t1` with `arab_t2`, we obtain an estimated ATE of 5.24. The two-tailed p-value for the latter coefficient is 0.028, which falls below the conventional 0.05 significance threshold. The estimated ATE remains substantively important and statistically distinguishable from zero.

```
> summary(lm(Y~condition+A+W, data=murrar))
Coefficients:
            Estimate Std. Error t value Pr(>|t|)
(Intercept) 23.64246    5.27981   4.478 1.48e-05 ***
condition    5.24420    2.36805   2.215   0.0283 *
A            0.53518    0.07665   6.982 8.79e-11 ***
W            0.08848    0.08286   1.068   0.2873
---
Signif. codes:  0 '***' 0.001 '**' 0.01 '*' 0.05 '.' 0.1 ' ' 1

Residual standard error: 14.63 on 150 degrees of freedom
  (39 observations deleted due to missingness)
Multiple R-squared: 0.4136,    Adjusted R-squared: 0.4018
F-statistic: 35.26 on 3 and 150 DF,  p-value: < 2.2e-16
```

References

Ansolabehere, Stephen, and Shanto Iyengar. 1995. *Going Negative: How Political Advertisements Shrink and Polarize the Electorate*. New York: Free Press.

Asha'ari, Zamzil Amin, Mohd Zaki Ahmad, Wan Shah Jihan Wan Din, Che Maraina Che Hussin, and Ishlah Leman. 2013. "Ingestion of honey improves the symptoms of allergic rhinitis: Evidence from a randomized placebo-controlled trial in the East coast of Peninsular Malaysia." *Annals of Saudi Medicine* 33(5): 469–475.

Baird, Sarah, Francisco H. G. Ferreira, Berk Özler, and Michael Woolcock. 2014. "Conditional, unconditional and everything in between: A systematic review of the effects of cash transfer programmes on schooling outcomes." *Journal of Development Effectiveness* 6(1): 1–43.

Baker, Shamin M., Otis W. Brawley, and Leonard S. Marks. 2005. "Effects of untreated syphilis in the negro male, 1932 to 1972: A closure comes to the Tuskegee study, 2004." *Urology* 65(6): 1259–1262.

Balcells, Laia, Valeria Palanza, and Elsa Voytas. 2022. "Do transitional justice museums persuade visitors? Evidence from a field experiment." *The Journal of Politics* 84(1): 496–510.

Baldassarri, Delia, and Maria Abascal. 2017. "Field experiments across the social sciences." *Annual Review of Sociology* 43: 41–73.

Banerjee, Abhijit, Eliana La Ferrara, and Victor H. Orozco-Olvera. 2019. "The entertaining way to behavioral change: Fighting HIV with MTV." NBER. Working paper.

Banerjee, Abhijit, and Esther Duflo. 2017. *Handbook of Field Experiments*, 1st ed. Amsterdam: North-Holland.

Banerjee, Abhijit, Selvan Kumar, Rohini Pande, and Felix Su. 2011. "Do informed voters make better choices? Experimental evidence from urban India." Unpublished manuscript.

Banikowski, Alison K., and Teresa A. Mehring. 1999. "Strategies to enhance memory based on brain research." *Focus On Exceptional Children* 32(2): 1–16.

Barber, Michael, and Jeremy C. Pope. 2019. "Does party trump ideology? Disentangling party and ideology in America." *The American Political Science Review* 113(1): 38–54.

Berinsky, Adam J., Gregory A. Huber, and Gabriel S. Lenz. 2012. "Evaluating online labor markets for experimental research: Amazon.com's Mechanical Turk." *Political Analysis* 20(3): 351–368.

Bertrand, Marianne, Simeon Djankov, Rema Hanna, and Sendhil Mullainathan. 2007. "Obtaining a driver's license in India: An experimental approach to studying corruption." *The Quarterly Journal of Economics* 122(4): 1639–1676.

Blair, Graeme, and Gwyneth McClendon. 2021. "Conducting experiments in multiple contexts." In *Advances in Experimental Political Science*, eds. James N. Druckman and Donald P. Green, 411–430. New York: Cambridge University Press.

Blass, Thomas. 2004. *The Man Who Shocked the World: The Life and Legacy of Stanley Milgram*. New York: Basic Books.

Broockman, David E., and Donald P. Green. 2014. "Do online advertisements increase political candidates' name recognition or favorability? Evidence from randomized field experiments." *Political Behavior* 36(2): 263–289.

Bruneau, Emile G., and Rebecca Saxe. 2012. "The power of being heard: The benefits of 'perspective-giving' in the context of intergroup conflict." *Journal of Experimental Social Psychology* 48(4): 855–866.

Burger, Jerry M. 2009. "Replicating Milgram: Would people still obey today?" *American Psychologist* 64(1): 1–11.

Butler, Daniel M., Christopher F. Karpowitz, and Jeremy C. Pope. 2012. "A field experiment on legislators' home styles: Service versus policy." *The Journal of Politics* 74(2): 474–486.

Chang, Edward H., Katherine L. Milkman, Dena M. Gromet, et al. 2019. "The mixed effects of online diversity training." *Proceedings of the National Academy of Sciences* 116(16): 7778–7783.

Chetty, Raj, Nathaniel Hendren, and Lawrence F. Katz. 2016. "The effects of exposure to better neighborhoods on children: New evidence from the moving to opportunity experiment." *American Economic Review* 106(4): 855–902.

Christensen, Larry. 1988. "Deception in psychological research: When is its use justified?" *Personality and Social Psychology Bulletin* 14(4): 664–675.

Clingingsmith, David, Asim I. Khwaja, and Michael Kremer. 2009. "Estimating the impact of the Hajj: Religion and tolerance in Islam's global gathering." *The Quarterly Journal of Economics* 124(3): 1133–1170.

Code of Federal Regulations. 2018. *Part 46: Protection of Human Subjects.* Available at: www.ecfr .gov/on/2018-07-19/title-45/subtitle-A/subchapter-A/part-46 (last accessed February 23, 2022).

Collazos, Daniela, Eduardo García, Daniel Mejía, Daniel Ortega, and Santiago Tobón. 2021. "Hot spots policing in a high-crime environment: An experimental evaluation in Medellin." *Journal of Experimental Criminology* 17(3): 473–506.

Committee on Ethical Standards in Psychological Research. 1973. "Ethical principles in the conduct of research with human participants." *American Psychologist* 28(1): 79–80.

Coppock, Alexander. 2021. "Visualize as you randomize." In *Advances in Experimental Political Science*, eds. James N. Druckman and Donald P. Green, 320–338. New York: Cambridge University Press.

Coppock, Alexander, and Oliver A. McClellan. 2019. "Validating the demographic, political, psychological, and experimental results obtained from a new source of online survey respondents." *Research & Politics* 6(1): 1–14.

Dawes, Robyn M. 2009. *House of Cards: Psychology and Psychotherapy Built on Myth*. New York: Free Press.

Desposato, Scott. 2015. *Ethics and Experiments: Problems and Solutions for Social Scientists and Policy Professionals*. Abingdon: Routledge.

Dickson, Eric S. 2011. "Economics versus psychology experiments." In *Cambridge Handbook of Experimental Political Science*, eds. James N. Druckman, Donald P. Green, Jame H. Kuklinski, and Arthur Lupia, 58–69. New York: Cambridge University Press.

Doleac, Jennifer L., and Luke C. Stein. 2013. "The visible hand: Race and online market outcomes." *The Economic Journal* 123(572): F469–F492.

Druckman, James, and Donald P. Green. 2021. *Advances in Experimental Political Science*. Cambridge: Cambridge University Press.

Dunning, Thad, Guy Grossman, Macartan Humphreys, et al. 2019. "Voter information campaigns and political accountability: Cumulative findings from a preregistered meta-analysis of coordinated trials." *Science Advances* 5(7): eaaw2612.

Egger, Dennis, Johannes Haushofer, Edward Miguel, Paul Niehaus, and Michael W. Walker. 2019. *General equilibrium effects of cash transfers: experimental evidence from Kenya*. No. w26600. National Bureau of Economic Research.

Ellison, Brenna, Olesya Savchenko, Cassandra J. Nikolaus, and Brittany R. L. Duff. 2019. "Every plate counts: Evaluation of a food waste reduction campaign in a university dining hall." *Resources, Conservation and Recycling* 144: 276–284.

Farrington, David P., Friedrich Losel, Anthony A. Braga, et al. 2020. "Experimental criminology: Looking back and forward on the 20th anniversary of the academy of experimental criminology." *Journal of Experimental Criminology* 16(4): 649–673.

Finkelstein, Amy, Sarah Taubman, Bill Wright, et al. 2012. "The Oregon health insurance experiment: Evidence from the first year." *The Quarterly Journal of Economics* 127(3): 1057–1106.

Fisher, Ronald A. 1926. "The arrangement of field experiments." *Journal of the Ministry of Agriculture* 33: 503–515.

Franco, Annie, Neil Malhotra, and Gabor Simonovits. 2014. "Publication bias in the social sciences: Unlocking the file drawer." *Science* 345(6203): 1502–1505.

Fried, Brian J., Paul Lagunes, and Atheendar Venkataramani. 2010. "Corruption and inequality at the crossroad: A multimethod study of bribery and discrimination in Latin America." *Latin American Research Review* 45(1): 76–97.

Frijters, Paul, Asad Islam, Chitwan Lalji, and Debayan Pakrashi. 2019. "Roommate effects in health outcomes." *Health Economics* 28(8): 998–1034.

Galiani, Sebastian, Martin Rossi, and Ernesto Schargrodsky. 2011. "Conscription and crime: Evidence from the Argentine Draft Lottery." *American Economic Journal: Applied Economics* 3(2): 119–136.

Gerber, Alan S., and Donald P. Green. 2012. *Field Experiments: Design, Analysis, and Interpretation.* New York: W. W. Norton.

Gerber, Alan S., and Eric M. Patashnik. 2006. "Sham surgery: The problem of inadequate medical evidence." In *Promoting the General Welfare: New Perspectives on Government Performance*, eds. Alan S. Gerber and Eric M. Patashnik, 43–73. Washington, DC: Brookings Institution Press.

Green, Donald P., and Alan S. Gerber. 2019. *Get Out the Vote: How to Increase Voter Turnout.* Washington, DC: Brookings Institution Press.

Green, Donald P., Dylan W. Groves, and Constantine Manda. 2021. "A radio drama's effects on HIV attitudes and policy priorities: A field experiment in tanzania." *Health Education & Behavior* 48(6): 842–851.

Green, Donald P., and Holger L. Kern. 2012. "Modeling heterogeneous treatment effects in survey experiments with Bayesian additive regression trees." *Public Opinion Quarterly* 76(3): 491–511.

Greiner, D. James, and Andrea Matthews. 2016. "Randomized control trials in the United States legal profession." *Annual Review of Law and Social Science* 12(1): 295–312.

Hainmueller, Jens, and Daniel J. Hopkins. 2015. "The hidden American immigration consensus: A conjoint analysis of attitudes toward immigrants." *American Journal of Political Science* 59(3): 529–548.

Hall, Andrew B., Connor Huff, and Shiro Kuriwaki. 2019. "Wealth, slaveownership, and fighting for the confederacy: An empirical study of the American civil war." *American Political Science Review* 113(3): 658–673.

Hayran, Ceren, Lalin Anik, and Zeynep Gürhan-Canli. 2020. "A threat to loyalty: Fear of missing out (FOMO) leads to reluctance to repeat current experiences." *PLoS ONE* 15(4): 1–17.

Humphreys, Macartan. 2015. "Reflections on the ethics of social experimentation." *Journal of Globalization and Development* 6(1): 87–112.

Iyengar, Shanto, Mark D. Peters, and Donald R. Kinder. 1982. "Experimental demonstrations of the 'not-so-minimal' consequences of television news programs." *The American Political Science Review* 76(4): 848–858.

Iyengar, Shanto, and Sean J. Westwood. 2015. "Fear and loathing across party lines: New evidence on group polarization." *American Journal of Political Science* 59(3): 690–707.

Kuhn, Peter, Peter Kooreman, Adriaan Soetevent, and Arie Kapteyn. 2011. "The effects of lottery prizes on winners and their neighbors: Evidence from the Dutch postcode lottery." *American Economic Review* 101(5): 2226–2247.

Lachin, John M. 2020. "Nonparametric statistical analysis." *JAMA* 323(20): 2080–2081.

Lacroix, Karine, and Robert Gifford. 2020. "Targeting interventions to distinct meat-eating groups reduces meat consumption." *Food Quality and Preference* 86: 103997.

Le Texier, Thibault. 2019. "Debunking the Stanford prison experiment." *American Psychologist* 74(7): 823.

Lynn, Michael. 2018. "Are published techniques for increasing service-gratuities/tips effective? P-curving and R-indexing the evidence." *International Journal of Hospitality Management* 69(1): 65–74.

Lynn, Michael and Kirby Mynier. 1993. "Effect of server posture on restaurant tipping 1." *Journal of Applied Social Psychology* 23(8): 678-685.

McClendon, Gwyneth, and Rachel B. Riedl. 2015. "Religion as a stimulant of political participation: Experimental evidence from Nairobi, Kenya." *The Journal of Politics* 77(4): 1045–1057.

McDermott, Rose, and Peter K. Hatemi. 2020. "Ethics in field experimentation: A call to establish new standards to protect the public from unwanted manipulation and real harms." *Proceedings of the National Academy of Sciences* 117(48): 30014–30021.

McGrath, Mary C., Peter M. Aronow, and Vivien Shotwell. 2016. "Chocolate scents and product sales: A randomized controlled trial in a Canadian bookstore and café." *SpringerPlus* 5(1): 1–6.

Michelson, Melissa R. 2016. "The risk of over-reliance on the institutional review board: An approved project is not always an ethical project." *PS, Political Science & Politics* 49(2): 299.

Milgram, Stanley. 1963. "Behavioral study of obedience." *The Journal of Abnormal and Social Psychology* 67(4): 371–378.

Milkman, K. L., Gromet, D., Ho, H., et al. 2021. "Megastudies improve the impact of applied behavioural science." *Nature* 600(7889): 478–483.

Moe, Angelica, and Rossana De Beni. 2005. "Stressing the efficacy of the loci method: Oral presentation and the subject-generation of the loci pathway with expository passages." *Applied Cognitive Psychology* 19(1): 95–106.

Morton, Rebecca B., and Kenneth C. Williams. 2010. *Experimental Political Science and the Study of Causality: From Nature to the Lab*. New York: Cambridge University Press.

Mousa, Salma. 2020. "Building social cohesion between christians and muslims through soccer in post-ISIS Iraq." *Science* 369(6505): 866–870.

Mullinix, Kevin J., Toby Bolsen, and Robert J. Norris. 2021. "The feedback effects of controversial police use of force." *Political Behavior* 43(2): 881–898.

Mummolo, Jonathan, and Erik Peterson. 2019. "Demand effects in survey experiments: An empirical assessment." *American Political Science Review* 113(2): 517–529.

Munger, Kevin. 2017. "Tweetment effects on the tweeted: Experimentally reducing racist harassment." *Political Behavior* 39(3): 629–649.

Murrar, Sohad, and Markus Brauer. 2018. "Entertainment-education effectively reduces prejudice." *Group Processes & Intergroup Relations* 21(7): 1053–1077.

Mutz, Diana C., and Byron Reeves. 2005. "The new videomalaise: Effects of televised incivility on political trust." *American Political Science Review* 99(1): 1–15.

National Commission for the Protection of Human Subjects of Biomedical and Behavioral Research. 1978. *The Belmont Report: Ethical Principles and Guidelines for the Protection of Human Subjects of Research*. Bethesda, MD: The Commission.

Nickerson, David W. 2008. "Is voting contagious? Evidence from two field experiments." *The American Political Science Review* 102(1): 49–57.

Ortmann, Andreas. 2019. "Deception." In *Handbook of Research Methods and Applications in Experimental Economics*, eds. Arthur Schram and Aljaz Ule, 28–38. Northampton, MA: Edward Elgar.

Osbaldiston, Richard, and John Paul Schott. 2012. "Environmental sustainability and behavioral science: Meta-analysis of proenvironmental behavior experiments." *Environment and Behavior* 44(2): 257–299.

Pager, Devah. 2007. "The use of field experiments for studies of employment discrimination: Contributions, critiques, and directions for the future." *Annals of the American Academy of Political and Social Science* 609(1): 104–133.

Paluck, Elizabeth Levy. 2009. "Reducing intergroup prejudice and conflict using the media: A field experiment in Rwanda." *Journal of Personality and Social Psychology* 96(3): 574.

Paluck, Elizabeth Levy, Roni Porat, Chelsey S. Clark, and Donald P. Green. 2021. "Prejudice reduction: Progress and challenges." *Annual Review of Psychology* 72: 533–560.

Panagopoulos, Costas. 2011. "Thank you for voting: Gratitude expression and voter mobilization." *The Journal of Politics* 73(3): 707–717.

Panagopoulos, Costas, Donald P. Green, Jonathan Krasno, Michael Schwam-Baird, and Kyle Endres. 2020. "Partisan consumerism: Experimental tests of consumer reactions to corporate political activity." *The Journal of Politics* 82(3): 996–1007.

Parigi, Paolo, Jessica J. Santana, and Karen S. Cook. 2017. "Online field experiments: Studying social interactions in context." *Social Psychology Quarterly* 80(1): 1–19.

Peisakhin, Leonid, and Paul Pinto. 2010. "Is transparency an effective anti-corruption strategy? Evidence from a field experiment in India." *Regulation & Governance* 4(3): 261–280.

de Quidt, Jonathan, Johannes Haushofer, and Christopher Roth. 2018. "Measuring and bounding experimenter demand." *American Economic Review* 108(11): 3266–3302.

Rajan, T. V., Howard Tennen, Richard L. Lindquist, Leonard Cohen, and J. Clive. 2002. "Effect of ingestion of honey on symptoms of rhinoconjunctivitis." *Annals of Allergy, Asthma & Immunology* 88(2): 198–203.

Raudenbush, Stephen W., and Daniel Schwartz. 2020. "Randomized experiments in education, with implications for multilevel causal inference." *Annual Review of Statistics and Its Application* 7(1): 177–208.

Rind, Bruce, and Prashant Bordia. 1996. "Effect on restaurant tipping of male and female servers drawing a happy, smiling face on the backs of customers' checks." *Journal of Applied Social Psychology* 26(3): 218–225.

Robitaille, Nicole, Nina Mazar, Claire I. Tsai, Avery M. Haviv, and Elizabeth Hardy. 2021. "Increasing organ donor registrations with behavioral interventions: A field experiment." *Journal of Marketing* 85(3): 168–183.

Rondeau, Daniel, and John A. List. 2008. "Matching and challenge gifts to charity: Evidence from laboratory and natural field experiments." *Experimental Economics* 11(3): 253–267.

Rosenthal, Sonny, and Noah Linder. 2021. "Effects of bin proximity and informational prompts on recycling and contamination." *Resources, Conservation and Recycling* 168: 105430.

Rousu, Matthew C., Gregory Colson, Jay R. Corrigan, Carlos Grebitus, and Mario Loureiro. 2015. "Deception in experiments: Towards guidelines on use in applied economics research." *Applied Economics: Perspectives and Policy* 37(3): 524–536.

Sawilowsky, Shlomo S., and Robert C. Blair. 1992. "A more realistic look at the robustness and type II error properties of the t test to departures from population normality." *Psychological Bulletin* 111(2): 352–360.

Schwam-Baird, Michael, Costas Panagopoulos, Jonathan S. Krasno, and Donald P. Green. 2016. "Do public matching funds and tax credits encourage political contributions? Evidence from three field experiments using nonpartisan messages." *Election Law Journal* 15(2): 129–142.

Sénémeaud, Cécile, Camille Sanrey, Nathalie Callé, et al. 2017. "The watching-eyes phenomenon and blood donation: Does exposure to pictures of eyes increase blood donation by young adults?" *Transfusion and Apheresis Science* 56(2): 168–170.

Shadish, William R., and Thomas D. Cook. 2009. "The renaissance of field experimentation in evaluating interventions." *Annual Review of Psychology* 60: 607–629.

Sherman, Lawrence W., and Dennis P. Rogan. 1995. "Deterrent effects of police raids on crack houses: A randomized, controlled experiment." *Justice Quarterly* 12(4): 755–781.

Siegel, Alexandra A., and Vivienne Badaan. 2020. "# No2Sectarianism: Experimental approaches to reducing sectarian hate speech online." *American Political Science Review* 114(3): 837–855.

Siemieniuk, Reed A. C., Ian A. Harris, Thomas Agoritsas, et al. 2017. "Arthroscopic surgery for degenerative knee arthritis and meniscal tears: A clinical practice guideline." *The BMJ*. Available at: www.bmj.com/content/357/bmj.j1982 (last accessed June 8, 2021).

Simonsohn, Uri, Leif D. Nelson, and Joseph P. Simmons. 2014. "P-curve: A key to the file-drawer." *Journal of Experimental Psychology: General* 143(2): 534.

Smith, Tom W. 1987. "That which we call welfare by any other name would smell sweeter." *The Public Opinion Quarterly* 51(1): 75–83.

Teschner, Florian, and Henner Gimpel. 2018. "Crowd labor markets as platform for group decision and negotiation research: A comparison to laboratory experiments." *Group Decision and Negotiation* 27(2): 197–214.

Tetlock, Philip E. 2017. *Expert Political Judgment: How Good Is it? How Can We Know?* Princeton, NJ: Princeton University Press.

Torgerson, David, and Carole J. Torgerson. 2008. *Designing Randomised Trials in Health, Education and the Social Sciences: An Introduction.* New York: Palgrave Macmillan.

Whitfield, Gregory. 2019. "Toward a separate ethics of political field experiments." *Political Research Quarterly* 72(3): 527–538.

Wren-Lewis, Liam, Luis Becerra-Valbuena, and Kenneth Houngbedji. 2020. "Formalizing land rights can reduce forest loss: Experimental evidence from Benin." *Science Advances* 6(26): 1–8.

Zhou, Alan, Yesenia Ruano, Kerem Tuncer, and Oscar Scott. July 2021. The Effect of Political Affiliation on Undergraduate Admissions Bias. Unpublished manuscript, Department of Political Science, Columbia University.

Zimbardo, Philip G. 1973. On the ethics of intervention in human psychological research: With special reference to the Stanford prison experiment. *Cognition* 2(2): 243–256.

Index